TRIATHLON

BIKE

FOUNDATIONS

A System for Every Triathlete to Finish the Bike
Feeling Strong and Ready to Nail the Run
with Just Two Workouts a Week!

"TRIATHLON TAREN" GESELL

ISBN: 978-1-6892-0922-9

Visit Amazon for other books by "TRIATHLON TAREN" GESELL

CONTENTS

CHAPTER 1

CLIPPING IN

INTRODUCTION

I remember the exact day I went out for my first training ride to get ready for my very first triathlon.

I had been training on stationary and spin bikes at the gym all winter, and during those rides, I visualized crushing the racecourse, passing athlete after athlete who got out of the water before me. I had biked everywhere as a kid, sometimes with a set of golf clubs or curling gear on my back, and I had strong legs from previous years of weightlifting before I got into triathlon. I figured the bike portion of my first race would be my time to shine.

Spring came around and I bought a road bike from a local shop plus an entry-level helmet, cycling shorts, and a jersey. I decided against cycling shoes, for the time being, keeping to my modest budget. When the snow finally melted a couple of months before my first race, I went out for my first real outdoor ride in 15 years. I was ready to tear the ride apart and get some motivation for that first race. But I couldn't have been more wrong in my visions of what that ride would be like.

Gusts of wind on the highway knocked me around like it was my first time on a bike (there hadn't been any wind on the indoor bikes at the gym). I crunched the gears every time I shifted and either bounced wildly on the saddle or felt like I was turning pedals through quicksand. After what felt like riding forever, I hit my turnaround point only to realize the wind had been at my back on the way out and now I had to push through the wind on my way home. My legs ached, and they could barely turn the pedals. I had to stop for several breaks.

When I got home, I thought I must have clocked the longest ride I'd ever done in my life. I used Google Maps to plot my route, expecting some astronomical distance. Instead, the route I plotted was a deflating 10 kilometers. Seriously, 10 kilometers. A measly six miles!! I was completely thrashed; my legs felt like Jell-O, I was walking funny, my lower back hurt, and my arms ached from getting knocked around in the wind. I had ridden at barely 20 km/h (12 mph) over 10 kilometers and it almost killed me. Suddenly, my upcoming race with a 13-kilometer bike followed by a run appeared impossible, and I thought my eventual goal of doing an IRONMAN with a 180 km ride was totally washed away.

I kept at my training, but the first race a couple of months later didn't go much better than my first-ever ride. It was a Try-a-Tri beginner race with a 300m swim, a 13 km bike, and a 3 km run. Sure enough, by the end of the bike, my legs didn't have any power left and when I hopped off the bike to start running, I almost fell over. Fifty strides into the run, my quads had cramped so much I was running like Frankenstein.

Despite that less-than-promising start, I stuck with it. Fast forward three years and the bike had become my strongest discipline in triathlon; I was able to complete a 20 km Sprint distance bike in just 32 minutes (average speed of 37.5 km/h or 23.3 mph). A couple of years later, I was able to ride and sprint with some of the best road cyclists in our province. And now, as I'm writing this, I recently clocked a high-of-a-lifetime, personal best bike split of 2:18 for 90 km in half-IRONMAN Puerto Rico (39.2 km/h or 24.36 mph), which was the sixth-fastest bike of the day of the 1200 triathletes who started the race.

The first assumption by a lot of people is that my improvement is simply thanks to bike upgrades, but as Lance Armstrong ironically said, "It's not about the bike." That's completely true. Those fast Sprint distance races were done on a $600 Cervelo P3 that had lived through a fire, and I qualified for the 2018 IRONMAN 70.3 World Championship on an entry-level Cervelo P2 with basic Shimano 105 components I borrowed from my local bike shop. Sure, having a nice bike helps but no bike could ever give you the kind of improvement I just described. In other words, you won't have to use up your children's college fund to buy a good enough bike to cycle well in triathlon.

In fact, when I made the most progress on the bike, I didn't do a lot of the things triathletes think are non-negotiable requirements to becoming a fast cyclist. I didn't do insanely long rides every weekend, I didn't have a coach, I didn't have a power meter, and I didn't have to diet down to some unhealthy, unsustainable body weight to get faster.

The process of my getting faster on the bike was very simple, and it's the system you're going to learn in this book:

1. Get the right gear that does NOT break the bank.
2. Do just two workouts a week, but make them the RIGHT workouts.
3. Design your training to make you strong on the bike.

With just these three key items addressed, you'll nail your power and pacing through wind, over hills, and past your competitors all the way to the end of the bike (and still be fresh for the run!) The bike will become an enjoyable part of your training and a weapon in your racing.

Finally, before getting into the good stuff, I've got even more good stuff for you at triathlontaren.com/bikefoundations where you should go right now and enter your email address so we can send you the calculators and tools that go along with this book. Sure, you could make the spreadsheets and calculations on your own, but we've already done all of the work for you so you can more spend time on your bike, which is the whole point, isn't it?

CHAPTER 2

YOU'VE GOT WHAT IT TAKES

You may have read the last chapter and thought to yourself, "This is great for you, Taren, but how am I supposed to believe it will work for me?" I know you'll be able to get faster on the bike because we see athletes—even top professionals—make improvements on the bike all the time.

Professional triathlete Lucy Charles' first triathlon ever was IRONMAN UK, a brutally hard course that she completed in 12:16 with a 6:55 bike split. This was just the third fastest bike in her age group. It certainly was not a screaming indication that she had any bike talent. Her second race was a half IRONMAN, where she won the age group but only had the second fastest bike in the age group of 2:50:04. Again, not so impressive. Now, in 2019, Lucy is ranked as one of the best bikers in the pro women's field. In the 2018 IRONMAN 70.3 World Championship, Daniela Ryf (70.3 and full IRONMAN World Champion, and one of the fastest female cyclists triathlon has ever seen), caught Lucy Charles on the bike but instead of being able to pass Lucy, Lucy held Daniela's wheel the entire ride!

Jan Frodeno, the 2008 Olympic gold medalist in triathlon, had spent an entire career competing in draft-legal races. These draft-legal events neutralize the bike, and because everyone rides in a pack, it doesn't reward strong cyclists so the athletes don't focus on sharpening their bike strength. Jan's first long course race was the 2013 70.3 European Championship, where he finished second overall, but in that race, he didn't even have one of the top 10 fastest bike splits. The next year, Jan made his full IRONMAN debut in Frankfurt where he clocked just the sixth-fastest bike split but was still a full 21 minutes behind the fastest rider of the day. Fast forward to 2017 and 2018, and Jan is now coming off the bike right up there with the superbikers, Sebastian Kienle, Lionel Sanders, Sam Appleton, and Cameron Wurf.

Progress on the bike can be made by any triathlete at any stage, whether you're starting as an age group amateur, a fit athlete coming from another sport, or an Olympic gold medalist who needs to improve on the bike. All it takes is the right training system.

Making progress on the bike is unlike swimming or running. In swimming, unless you're given the exact right prescription to develop proper technique, triathletes often swim for years without making any progress. And it's even harder to make progress in running because it's very dependent on an athlete's biomechanics and physiology; some people are built to run (see: springy tendoned Kenyans with feather-light calves) while others might struggle for an entire lifetime to make running feel smooth. With biking, however, it's almost a straight correlation between time spent in the saddle and improvements.

If you ride more, you will get faster; I guarantee it. The hurdle preventing a lot of triathletes from making progress on the bike is the belief that "ride more" means hours and hours away from work and family. Sure, long rides will help you get faster and stronger but with the right system, you won't need to put in hundreds and hundreds of hours over thousands of miles of riding to see improvements. Instead of careless cycle training, you're going to learn how to optimize your bike, your training, and your body so that with 100 percent certainty, you will get faster on the bike without getting a divorce or getting fired from your job because you have to spend so much time training.

WHAT IT TAKES

Before getting into the system of bike optimization that you're going to learn, we need to put into perspective how this system fits into what you've heard before about work and optimization. The buzzwords everyone hears today always fall into one of two buckets at opposite ends of a spectrum. Those two buckets are "hacks" and "hustle."

"Hacks" are shortcuts, cheats, and quicker ways to get where you want to be. In triathlon, this reads like, "10 Weeks to an IRONMAN Personal Best" or "Get 30 Seconds Faster Per Mile with This One Fix." These messages lead people to believe there's some secret method that triathletes and coaches don't know about, but that the guru supporting the idea does, and that will instantly allow you to make improvements without work.

"Hustle," on the other hand, is the exact opposite message and supports a constant effort, huge workloads, and never taking a break. In triathlon, this looks like the Instagrammers who post about their 4:30 a.m. swims, their constant workouts despite fatigue/stress/soreness, and their motivational quotes claiming, "If you want it bad enough you have to be willing to suffer." I feel these messages lead triathletes to believe that the only way to be a triathlete is to constantly train and suffer through hard hours away from family and real-life commitments.

I think both messages are disingenuous and lead to unhealthy approaches (and outcomes) for triathletes.

"Hack"-thinking results in inconsistent performance. Athletes who are looking for hacks might not train enough to be well-prepared for their race. They tend to be looking for a "secret" to unlock training that will propel them to great performances in half the time, and they often bounce from training method to training method without ever committing to one thing long enough to absorb the benefits. Finally, they tend to come into races thinking this "secret" to training and racing is going to result in amazing performances, setting expectations very high and hard-to-reach.

This isn't to say there aren't ways that you can optimize your training; we're going to talk a lot about how you can get the most out of the time you spend training so you don't have to put in hundreds of mindless hours. But taking the approach of performing *effective* training is very different from *hacking* your training.

Hustle, in my opinion, is far more dangerous, particularly for triathletes. The concept of "No Pain, No Gain" and "If you want it bad enough you'll make the necessary sacrifices" might be fine for professional athletes who can choose to risk their overall health for the potential reward of greatness in a sport and a lifetime of income, but for the amateur triathlete, suffering through training can lead to serious negative long-term health consequences. I think the "SHUT UP AND DO WORK!" approach has no business for amateurs in our sport.

Dr. Dan Plews, a sports scientist, coach to three professional triathletes who have gone under eight hours in the IRONMAN distance, and himself the 2018 overall amateur champion and course record-holder at the IRONMAN World Championship in Kona, told me that when he started working with professional triathletes he looked at their fast training and thought, "That's not that much faster than what I can do," but then he realized the difference between him and those elite professionals was that they have a huge amount more training than he does at the very easy efforts. As Dan puts it, "The difference between age groupers and pros is that when pros train, they go SO easy."

Why then do we see nothing but triathletes smashing themselves on social media? In the case of professional triathletes, I think it's just more fun to post "RUBBER LEGS after 12x1 km at 3:10/km with just 60 seconds rest between. Now time for a 7 km recovery swim. #ironmantraining" than it is to post, "Four hour really easy ride with five pee stops and listened to two Joe Rogan podcasts!" But when it comes to amateur triathletes, I think most simply don't know that the vast majority of training should be at very low, unimpressive intensity levels with just a tiny little amount of their training being quite challenging.

The topic of optimizing your training so you don't spend any more time training than you need to, by creating proper balance between hard work and easier effort, will be addressed in a separate resource I'm working on. For now, all you need to understand is that after seeing athlete after athlete, study after study, and talking to coach after coach, I've learned that the best results you'll get are when you combine a small amount of challenging training with a lot of easy training, balancing that with a lot of recovery and eating healthy, nourishing food. Put all of these factors together and you'll get faster every single year.

Each triathlete needs to choose an appropriate number of things to try to tackle for their unique situation, and to make sure that whatever time they can spend training is optimized so every minute is designed to get the maximum result possible. Every athlete can purchase only the amount of gear they can afford, perform only the number of workouts they can manage to balance with life, and still make great gains and get to a race as prepared as they can personally be.

The differences from one athlete to another might be in the amount of gear they can buy. Purchase a lot of gear and you'll be more aero than if you purchase none. Or you might be able to train for 15 hours a week while most triathletes are only training 6-9 hours a week. If that training is designed well, you'll probably be faster from the additional hours you've put in. But the key thing to remember in triathlon is this: if you're racing as an amateur, whether you finish first in your age group or 50th in your age group, we're all making the same amount of money (as in, none!) so you might as well enjoy it no matter what your life situation allows you to commit to in triathlon.

Don't stress about feeling like you always need to buy more and more gear that you can't afford or perform more and more training that you can't fit in. Do what's comfortable for you!

In this book, we'll talk about three things that are critical to starting on the right track with bike triathlon training:

1. We'll optimize your bike,
2. We'll optimize just two critical workouts you need to perform each week, and
3. We'll optimize your strength so you can finish the bike as fast as you started and be ready to have a great run.

OPTIMIZE YOUR BIKE

In this section, we're not going to tell you that you need to spend $15,000 on every last piece of gear that you could buy to make your bike as fast as possible. (Of course, you can purchase speed and if you have the money to do so, go for it! Buying bike gear is fun!)

Instead, what we'll do in this section is rank the order in which bike upgrades can be made, the approximate cost of each upgrade, and what benefit you'll get from the upgrade. You'll be able to select the upgrades you feel are worth your time and money so that no matter how much you want to invest in triathlon, you'll be set up in the best way possible to commit to the sport.

OPTIMIZE TWO WORKOUTS A WEEK

In this section, we'll tell you about the only two required rides that you need to do to perform well in whatever distance triathlon you want to tackle. When it comes right down to it, to bike well in our races we need to be able to bike fast for a long period. We're going to address the one workout a week you'll do to build speed and the other workout you'll do to build endurance.

Forget having to take time away from your family for months on end or setting up a stationary bike at your desk so you can get in extra three-hour rides while at work. With just two rides a week, done with the right structure, you can become VERY fast.

OPTIMIZE YOUR STRENGTH

In this section, we'll talk about how to make sure the speed and endurance you'll have built into your two workouts a week can be transferred to the race course, regardless of the conditions.

Your body will be strong enough to make sure you don't get sore while holding the aero position. Your legs will have the muscular endurance to pedal strong from the start of the bike to the end. You'll be able to ride in the hills and the wind and not have it suck the energy out of your legs. And you'll know how to pace the bike every step of the way, for every distance.

Put this together, perform the work we recommend, and you'll be able to settle into a nice comfortable aero position, be comfortable on your saddle, and hammer away on the bike portion of every race you do, holding strong speed and power until the end of the ride and getting off the bike ready to have the run of your life.

Let's get rolling, Trainiacs!

CHAPTER 3

OPTIMIZE YOUR BIKE

YOUR BIKE

Bike purchases are equally fun and stressful. The amount of bike gear triathletes can geek out on is endless; it's hard to "buy speed" in the pool or on the run, but you can always spend $700 on a new aero suit to save a few watts on the bike or put on one-time-use cotton race tires and latex tubes to reduce the rolling resistance on the road surface. And, of course, EVERYONE needs a power meter or they're basically not training, right? Nope!

These purchases are fun and if you have the funds to make these upgrades, by all means, go for it. Money spent on a bike will result in faster bike times. But do triathletes NEED to spend huge amounts of money on their bikes? Absolutely not.

For years, I rode a Cervelo P3 that cost me just $600 because it had been in a fire. The bike was supposed to be white, but the clearcoat over the white paint became yellowed thanks to the heat of the fire so the bike turned kind of yellow, the color of custard. (Fun fact: When I raced away from home, I told my competitors it was custom and they were super impressed). I bought a set of old deep Zipp race wheels for $400 that were cheap because the guy who put on the tubular tires added so much extra glue that dripped everywhere, and they were a total mess. I didn't have a race helmet, a fancy kit or a power meter, yet I was one of the stronger riders in any race I went to.

At the 2012 Subaru Banff Sprint Triathlon, a very competitive race because it was a qualifier for Worlds, I had the 10th fastest bike out of 360 athletes. In my first half-IRONMAN (70.3) distance race, the Duluth Superiorman, I had the 18th fastest bike out of 166 athletes despite only having done one ride at 90 km or longer.

When I finally moved on from this bike, I didn't buy a fancy superbike. I borrowed an entry-level Cervelo P2 with Shimano 105 components (the entry-level) from the local bike shop and on this entry-level bike, I was still able to race fast enough to qualify for the half-IRONMAN World Championships.

The speed and performance difference between a mountain bike or general city bike and a road bike is large, the difference between a road bike and a road bike with clip-on aerobars is large, and the difference between a road bike with clip-on aerobars and an entry-level tri bike is large. But once you get into even an entry-level tri bike, the marginal gains you'll get from making upgrades is small; even a $2,000 tri bike with a decent set of wheels will generally perform just as well as a $10,000 bike with electronic shifting, a power meter, and a disc wheel.

All this is to say that no matter where you're at in triathlon, whether you're just getting into the sport or you're fully committed to the sport but don't have a ton of money to spend on a bike, literally ride whatever bike is most easily accessible to you.

If all you have is a friend's mountain bike, ride it! Don't feel embarrassed; you'll walk into transition with that bike on race morning, and I guarantee you'll see other people with the same bike.

If you've got an old road bike from a friend, ride it! You'll benefit from some clip-on aerobars, but if your friend isn't cool with you slapping some clip-ons onto their bike or you can't spend a lot of time riding with the aerobars to get comfortable with them, don't worry about it and just ride the bike normally.

Maybe you've got a tri bike, but it doesn't have deep wheels, electronic shifting, cotton race tires, etc..., etc..., etc... RIDE IT ANYWAY!

When you first got your driver's license as a kid, you drove whatever car you had access to. Sometimes that meant borrowing your parents' minivan, or you saved up $300 for an unsafe 1986 Pontiac Acadian like me, or maybe you had a family member to buy a car for you. Whatever the case was, it didn't matter what you were driving because you were driving! Bikes and triathlon are the same, it doesn't matter what you have access to as long as you're doing triathlon. Nobody at the finish line asks what bike you were riding, so ride ANYTHING.

Of course, more expensive bikes will be faster, more aerodynamic, lighter, shift a little more quickly and precisely, but spending money you can't afford on a superbike is not a prerequisite for triathlon. Having fun, and not stressing out about your bike is a prerequisite for triathlon.

What I'll provide you in the next chapter is a progression of what bikes and upgrades you should make depending on your particular budget so you can decide how much bike you want to buy, and beyond that point, just enjoy the fact you're riding! There are very few things we can do as adults that are just as fun as when we were kids. Riding a bike is one of those things, so have a blast and don't stress.

MAKING UPGRADES

Let's get rolling on optimizing your bike to be as fast as possible given your particular budget and commitment level to triathlon. One last thing before we get into it: get a helmet before you even get a bike. (**NOTE: If you don't mind spending a little more money on your first helmet, go down to upgrade #7 below to learn more about helmets.)

A helmet is your most important piece of bike gear and should be your very first purchase. Take care of your brain!

REQUIRED PURCHASES

1. CITY/TRAIL/MOUNTAIN/WALMART-TYPE BIKE $0 - $500

As mentioned, when you're just getting into triathlon you can use whatever bike you have access to.

2. AEROBARS

Next, even if you're using an $80 Walmart bike, you will benefit from adding clip-on aerobars. Getting aerodynamic is a very important thing because, as fun as buying speed with bike gear is, approximately 80-85 percent of the total drag you have to push through is caused by your body, not your bike. A pair of clip-on aerobars will make your total frontal area smaller and you'll fight the wind much less.

The aerobars I like to recommend have a bend upward so your arms don't have to bend down to reach them; bending down creates tension in the upper body, tiring you out and leading to cramping once you get on the run. The inward bend of these types of aerobars will also allow your hands to sit in a neutral position instead of having to turn your palms upward to hold the bars firmly. It doesn't have to be the Profile Design aerobars shown below, but this is the general shape you're looking for.

When you first get a set of aerobars, even if you've been professionally fit on your bike, don't expect it to feel good. The triathlon aero position is quite unnatural and extreme, so it will take some getting used to. Start by holding the aero position just one or two minutes at a time, then gradually build up. As long as your bike position is good, you'll be as comfortable in the aero position as you are in the regular riding position within a few months.

3. ROAD BIKE

If you already have a road bike and you bypassed the Walmart bike stage, great! Go get yourself some aerobars and slap them on the bike to get started. Or if you've already done a bunch of training on the Walmart bike with aerobars, see if you can transfer those aerobars over to the new road bike.

I recommend buying a road bike before a triathlon bike for a few reasons:

A road bike is easier to handle than a tri bike and you'll develop better bike handling skills as a result. This will result in you being able to steer your bike straighter, whether it's a road bike or your eventual tri bike, essentially shortening your race course.

You can ride in a group or do a triathlon on a road bike, but you can't ride in a group safely on a tri bike. Triathlon bikes are much twitchier, they don't handle as well as road bikes, and if someone riding in a group drops into their aerobars, it's a big danger to the other riders (DO NOT drop into aerobars when you're riding in a group).

Road bikes are easier to resell than tri bikes, and despite what you think right now, you'll positively, without question, move on from the first bike you buy at some point so you'll want to be able to resell the bike easily (more on this right away).

Most people who purchase their first road bike have a budget of $1,000-$2,500. This price point has some unique requirements that other price points don't. Most triathletes who get their first bike want a brand new, shiny bike that they can call their own, but new bikes at this price point are so entry-level that they'll end up costing you more in the long run.

New bikes at the $1,000-$2,500 price point are entry-level bikes, often with Shimano 105 components, which have typically been some of the heaviest components to ride with (although recent updates have made them comparable to some slightly higher-priced components.) These bikes are also going to be the hardest bikes to resell for two reasons: LOTS of athletes buy these entry-level bikes, then they either upgrade their bikes or they leave the sport so there are a lot of used bikes being sold at this price-point. Also, as I said before, those who are buying bikes in this price range want something shiny and new so when you try to resell your entry-level bike, it's like trying to sell a square peg to a round hole. When you roll a new entry-level bike out of the bike shop, it can depreciate by 50 percent in a few seconds. In the order of most-to-least important, here's what I would look for in your first purchased bike:

Buy a used bike and let someone else pay for the depreciation. The day before I wrote this, I gave this advice to an old friend who was buying his first bike and he found a barely-ridden bike for $1,900 that was $5,000 brand new.

Buy a bike with Shimano Ultegra, Dura Ace, or SRAM Red components (also known as a groupsets or groupo). These components are a step up from entry-level components, and they're something that discerning bike buyers will be looking for.

Look for 11-speed instead of 10, or, heaven forbid, 9-speed. It's the standard as of 2019 and for the foreseeable future.

If possible, lean toward buying a bike with disc brakes. Disc brakes aren't very common as of writing this in early 2019, but they're becoming more common and within a few years people will be looking for them the same way they look for Ultegra components or better.

Lastly, look for a bike that has a chain and cassette (the gears on the back wheel) that look shiny and not black. A black chain is a dirty chain and it shows that if the seller won't even clean up the bike to sell it, the maintenance of the bike might not have been great. But, I put this as the last point because a dirty bike is not necessarily a bad bike to purchase; you'll be getting it dirty again in no time, and things like chains, cassettes, etc. can all be cleaned and they eventually get replaced anyway.

If your budget is beyond the entry-level bike and into the multiple thousands of dollars, ignore what I just said because you'll probably want to buy your bike from a local shop. As you start getting into higher-end bikes, they require more specialized parts and maintenance. Bike wrenching on high-end bikes is not common sense, so having a good relationship with a local bike shop will help you learn how to care for and adjust your bike.

One last thing, I love Ventum bikes and think they're great, but the differences in performance from one bike brand to the next are marginal. What I recommend when you're selecting a bike brand is to use the 2018 Kona Bike count below, and select a bike from one of the top 10 most common brands. Choosing a common bike makes it more likely that your bike shop sells the brand, knows how to work on the bike, and will have easier access to parts. As much as I like riding my Ventum, building it up with my local bike shop was a struggle at the start because every aspect of the build was a learning experience. This is what will happen regularly if you choose to purchase a unique bike brand.

The top 10 most common bikes at the 2018 IRONMAN World Championship:

BIKES

> Cervelo – 487
>
> Trek – 256
>
> Specialzed – 189
>
> Felt – 185
>
> Canyon – 130
>
> Argon 18 – 118

Scott – 110

BMC – 108

QR – 97

Giant - 92

If you choose to build a relationship with a local bike shop that sells one of the above brands, you'll likely never have an issue with your bike that they can't fix.

4. CLIP-IN PEDALS AND SHOES $200 - $300

Clip-in pedals are one of the first things a new cyclist or triathlete should look into getting for several reasons.

The first reason you should make an upgrade to clip-in pedals a priority is because of safety. Of course, you're likely going to fall the first time you wear clip-in pedals on a ride. Don't worry, it's a rite of passage. Once you get the hang of using clip-in pedals, they're much safer as you're better connected to your bike. You've only got three contact points with a bike: the pedals, the seat, and the handlebars, and you want to optimize your connection with the bike at each of these points. We can't clip you into the handlebars or seat, but you can be clipped into the pedals to be more stable on the bike.

Second, there's some debate about whether clip-in pedals result in a more efficient pedaling stroke than flat pedals. I fall into the pro clip-in pedal camp because I look at efficiency as "Putting as much force into the pedals as you can without force leaking out of the pedals." A study[1] was done to determine the amount of force a foot needed to exert at the same power for both flat and clip-in pedals. What was found was that to generate the same power (watts), the feet without clip-in pedals had to exert much more force. This goes to show that clip-in pedals are more efficient at transferring power into the pedals.

You'll hear that clip-in pedals allow you to pull up on the back side of the pedal stroke as the opposite foot is pressing down. This is REALLY hard to do. Even elite tour cyclists have been tested and found that they don't pull up on the back of the pedal stroke; instead, they're just pressing down on their foot less than age group riders do. So don't stress about pulling up on the pedal stroke.

I haven't come across much data showing the specific speed advantage of clip-in pedals over flats; it's highly debated around the Internet, but if you can be safer, more stable on your bike, put more power into the pedals and feel more confident because you look like a seasoned rider, then I'd say this is a no-brainer upgrade. You can see a bit of subjective data that Global Cycling Network produced if you YouTube search *"Clipless Pedals Vs Flat Pedals - Which Is Faster? | GCN Does Science."*

---

[1] https://www.ncbi.nlm.nih.gov/pmc/articles/PMC3666464/

5. BIKE FIT $200 - $300

Roughly 80-85 percent of the total drag triathletes need to overcome is from the body, not the bike. All the aerodynamic wind tunnel figures that bike companies like to report to get you to buy their latest and greatest model, pales in comparison to the advantage you can get by becoming more aerodynamic and comfortable in that aerodynamic position.

Getting a set of clip-on aerobars won't help you much if they're positioned in such a way that creates discomfort and you can't stay in the time trial position (aero position, or triathlon position we ride in). Getting used to the TT position takes a lot of time. Expect it to take months before you feel confident handling the bike and staying in the TT position for a long time. A bike fit that is suitable for your flexibility, back mobility, age and race distance, will allow you to avoid discomfort and adjust to the time trial position quicker and transfer more power into the pedals.

A road bike has less variability than a tri bike when it comes to bike fit options. The reason for this is that the triathlon position is much more severe on the body, so it needs to be highly optimized. All bikes can achieve an improved position with a bike fit; maybe it's a better hip angle, maybe it's a better saddle position, a cleat angle that works better for your knees, or a set of insoles that let your legs track in a straighter line.

Being comfortable in the time-trial position so that you can a) get into the position b) stay in that position for hours on end c) effectively transfer power to the pedal stroke and d) get off the bike without feeling like you just lost a hammer fight is critical to having a successful race. A proper bike fit will save you potentially 1-3 kilometers per hour on the bike, and maybe even more time on the run.

6. FITTED TRI SUIT $100 - $500

"If I had a thousand dollars to spend on making myself faster on the bike, I'd spend the first $700 of it on my body." This is what 2017 and 2018 IRONMAN Kona bike course record holder told us in our "How to Bike with Cam Wurf" course at protriathlontraining.com.

Further to the point about the bike fit upgrade and the fact that 80-85 percent of the total drag we need to overcome is generated from our body and not the bike, we need to make the body as slippery as possible.

You don't need to spend hundreds and hundreds of dollars on a super fancy high-end custom tri suit like pros have, but you should purchase gear that fits you snuggly so there's no loose fabric flopping around, and comfortably so that you don't chafe.

I recommend the first bit of kit you purchase is a pair of tight-fitting tri shorts and a tight-fitting cycling top. This mix-match, one-two combo will get you through both training and racing, reducing the amount of new kit you need to buy.

Men's or Women's Tri Suit: Nothing baggy, everything is tight to the skin.

The main difference between cycling shorts and tri shorts is that tri shorts have a smaller chamois so you don't have a soggy diaper when you finish the swim, but they're still comfortable enough to be used during training rides (whereas cycling shorts can't be used for both training rides and triathlons because of the diaper butt).

The main difference between a cycling top and a tri top is that a cycling top will have larger pockets and typically be a little less tight. If you get a nice, highly fitted cycling top, you'll have nice big pockets and fabric on the shoulders for all your training rides, and you'll be aero for your race. If you get a true tri top without the sleeves, it's less ideal for your training rides. If you use a cycling top for your race and the race is a non-wetsuit swim, you'll want to swim without the cycling top on as the pockets will create drag and slow you down (practice putting on your cycling top with a wet torso so you're comfortable doing it on race day).

Lastly, when choosing between long-sleeved and sleeveless tri suits, the decision comes down to your preference. Sleeveless tri suits are more comfortable but sleeved tri suits keep some of the sun off your skin, and the fabric is more aerodynamic than skin. If you want the most aero suit possible, you want a sleeved tri suit.

Expect a gain of 1-2 km per hour over baggy fitting clothes. Remember, you have to wear something on the bike, so you may as well buy something proper regardless of the speed advantage. The tips above will optimize your kit.

BONUS PURCHASES

Once you've got the basic bike setup in place from the list above, you can start considering some of these upgraded purchases that will give a good return on your money.

1. AERO HELMET $150 - $350

An aero helmet is likely the best dollar-for-speed purchase you can make. The speed advantage of an aero helmet over a traditional road cycling helmet is roughly 1 km per hour, but that comes with a big caveat. An aero helmet only provides this big advantage if you can stay in the aero position and not shift your head around; traditional aero helmets have a long tail behind your head that creates drag when you turn your head. Turn your head a lot (most triathletes do) and the long tail aero helmet could be a disadvantage.

I recommend the first "aero helmet" triathletes purchase is a combination aero-road helmet that is more aerodynamic than a traditional road helmet, but more user-friendly and forgiving than a long tail aero helmet.

Examples of these helmets are the Lazer Bullet, the Specialized S-Works Evade, the Bontrager Ballista, and the Giro Vanquish. These types of helmets provide a great advantage over traditional road helmets, aren't terribly slower than a long tail aero helmet (and are often faster for athletes who move around a lot), and you can wear these helmets during training and racing so you only need one helmet.

2. CLEAN UP BIKE BUILD $100 - $300

This is a very overlooked aspect of bike speed. Triathletes often spend thousands of dollars on a bike that's super aerodynamic and has all the wind tunnel data to prove it, then they mindlessly slap a bunch of water bottles, saddlebags, bento boxes and gels to the frame, completely ruining a lot of the aerodynamic gains that bike manufacturers have been making over the past two decades.

Spend a little bit of money to clean up your bike with some of the following ideas:

- Zip tie cables together while still allowing them to function.
- Take your bottles off the frame and get a bottle cage that goes horizontal between your arms on the aerobars or at a 45-degree angle in behind your saddle. (Note: I don't recommend an aerobar bottle that hangs way down under the aerobars vertically because if such a bottle is not properly integrated into your bike, it will act as a wind catch and result in poor bike handling.)
- Purchase an aero bento box to carry your nutrition.
- Remove all unnecessary parts (reflectors, stickers, etc.)

These small purchases can add up to as much as another ½ - 1 km per hour, depending on your starting point.

3. AERO WHEELS $1,000 - $4,000

A set of deep-section wheels that are 50mm deep or deeper will add roughly 1 km per hour to your bike speed at the same effort, but they're much more expensive than the other upgrades listed already. There are also some serious things to consider with wheel upgrades.

Pro triathlete Cameron Wurf's bike with approximately 80mm wheels.

All other things being equal, the best combination of wheels is a disc wheel on the rear and an 80mm or deeper wheel on the front. If you weigh more than 160 pounds (72 kgs), are a good bike handler (can ride easily on a painted line in the road without swerving back and forth), and bike close to or faster than 35 km/h, this is the combination for you.

If, however, you weigh less than 160 pounds, the disc wheel and deep section wheel in the front might cause you to get blown around and actually be slower with these deep wheels. If you're riding slower than 35 km/h, the disc wheel won't have much more benefit than a 60mm wheel. And if you can't ride a bike straight, it means you're unstable on the bike and winds will blow you around even more with these deep wheels.

You have to be a very confident rider for a rear disc and a deep front wheel to provide a clear benefit; otherwise, you might be spending a lot of extra money.

Instead, a likely better option for a lot of athletes is a deep section 80mm wheel in the rear and a 40-60mm wheel in the front. This is the standard configuration for pros in Kona. Cameron Wurf set his first Kona bike course record on a 60mm rear wheel and a 40mm front wheel because his history as a professional cyclist taught him that the most important thing with wheel selection is having a set of wheels that still allows you to ride in a straight line.

4. TRI BIKE $2,000 - $15,000

Notice how I still haven't mentioned getting a triathlon bike? That's because a tri bike will perform better in a race than a road bike, but the choice between racing on a road bike versus a tri bike isn't as simple as, "A tri bike is faster, therefore, buy a tri bike."

The benefits of a triathlon bike over a road bike to do triathlon are:

> ➤ Tri bikes are typically more adjustable so you can customize the fit of the bike better, be more comfortable, and stay in the aero position longer.

> ➢ The saddle of a tri bike is moved forward so it's more directly over top of the pedals. This opens up your hip angle thus working the quads and the glutes more evenly so that when you get off the bike, you can run better.
> ➢ Tri bikes are often designed with integrated flat pack or nutrition storage areas.

But a tri bike is a very specific bike that you won't be able to safely ride in a group. They're rigid and harder on the body. I compare sitting on a tri bike to sitting on a 2x4. And because there are fewer triathletes than there are pure cyclists, tri bikes will be harder to resell if you decide you don't want to continue with triathlon.

I recommend people buy a tri bike only once they know for certain they are going to continue doing triathlons for years to come. If you're still in the first couple years of triathlon and dancing on the fence between continuing with triathlons or not, but you're enjoying buying all the gear we've listed above, just ask your local bike shop to only recommend upgrades that you'd easily be able to move from your road bike to the tri bike.

If you pick away at some smaller upgrades early on and make certain those upgrades can be transferred over to a tri bike, when you finally get that tri bike, you'll have a complete set up that's about as aero as possible.

One final note, an entry-level tri bike with Ultegra components or better and the upgrades we've listed above (which will only set you back around $3,000), is going to be every bit as good for you as a $15,000 bike. The difference in performance between the $3,000 bike and the $15,000 is not very significant besides a few watts here or there; beyond $5,000, upgrades are luxury purchases that only provide tiny, incremental gains in performance. The upgrades listed above are significant in performance.

EVENTUAL PURCHASES

HEART RATE MONITOR vs. POWER METER

Most athletes think a power meter is a prerequisite for proper bike training. This is flat out wrong.

I trained only with a heart rate monitor until my seventh year in triathlon and I still made huge bike gains just by amassing time in the saddle. More often than not during those seven years, I didn't look at my heart rate during bike training and only paid attention to perceived exertion. In fact, I would encourage athletes to delay getting a power meter until they develop strong body awareness through heart rate and perceived exertion training. Learning your effort levels through the signals your body is giving you is a deadly tool to have in your tool kit on race day (more on this later when we talk about pacing).

A local sports scientist named Daryl Hurrie, who has coached Olympians and many high-performance athletes, said on our *Triathlon Taren* podcast that he wouldn't recommend new or developing triathletes get a power meter early on because they need to learn the signals of their body first. He said heart rate is a great tool that doesn't get the respect it deserves. Two-time IRONMAN Kona bike course record holder Cam Wurf doesn't monitor his power when he races; he recommends heart rate for race pacing.

Need even more evidence that you don't need to stress about getting a power meter? I once got to hang out at the Purple Patch Fitness pro triathlon camp where some of the best triathletes in the world like Sam Appleton, Sarah Piampiano, and a dozen other pros were laying down watts. Head coach Matt Dixon was calling out the bike workout before the pros pushed off and he did not give out one power number, one training zone, or one metric whatsoever. Instead, he gave these elite athletes effort levels such as, "You're going to go for 30 minutes at a hard effort, then end with a very hard effort." One pro, who was new to the group, said, "What percentage of FTP should the very hard effort be?" Matt replied, "It's a very hard effort," not even acknowledging the question about FTP (which stands for Functional Threshold Power).

One of the reasons that a power meter is overhyped is because it's such a fixed metric where training is based on a one-time FTP measurement. Let's say you do an FTP test that results in an FTP of 200 watts, and you create your training zones off this FTP number that says your speed and power building efforts should be around 200-240 watts. But what happens when you've got a speed and power building workout on a day when you've got some underlying sickness that you didn't have during the FTP test? You might push to get into that 200-240 range and make yourself sicker. On the flip side, what if you've had a few nights of excellent sleep and had been eating well for days, and during the speed and power building workout you could have actually pushed to 240-260 but you held yourself back because your zones said 200-240? In that case, you've robbed yourself of a great chance for an increased training effect.

Power meters are a great tool, and by all means, if you are a total data junkie, go ahead and get one. However, getting a power meter does not mean you don't have to learn your perceived effort levels, how to manage your heart rate, or learn how to be more fluid with your training beyond what set FTP-based training zones prescribe.

I feel a good heart rate monitor such as a Garmin chest strap or a Wahoo Tickr is a much better investment for a developing triathlete. Don't worry about the athletes who look down their noses at you for not training with power.

One final note: I don't recommend using the wrist-based heart rate monitors that are built into some watches these days. These heart rate monitors are wildly inaccurate by as much as 20-30 beats per minute in my experience.

POWER METER vs. INDOOR TRAINER

The next most common question I get is whether athletes should get a power meter or a good indoor bike trainer. My answer is always: whatever gets you riding more.

If you live in a cold or wet climate, or traffic and roads where you live are rough, then an indoor bike trainer is the way to go. If you always ride outside anyway and the indoor trainer will collect dust, then get a power meter instead.

Neither a power meter nor a bike trainer will be the tool that makes or breaks your training. What will make or break your training is the amount of riding you do. So, get whichever tool allows you to ride more.

WHEN TO GET A POWER METER

The proper time to get a power meter is: whenever you want one… as long as you've first developed the ability to train and race *without* one. If you feel you need a power meter to help pace your races, that's a perfect reason to not get a power meter because you still need to develop the effort awareness to pace your race—in other words, you need to be able to feel your pacing without the help of a gadget. Proper race pacing involves more perceived exertion than power number monitoring.

My fastest ever Sprint bike and overall race time was done without any data whatsoever and totally by feel. The Austin IM 70.3 race, when I qualified for the 2018 70.3 World

Championship, was done without a power meter because it died in the cold conditions that day.

If you *need* a power meter to monitor your effort levels, you're not ready for one. Only get a power meter once you've developed the awareness of training efforts.

BASIC INDOOR TRAINER vs. SMART TRAINER

The time to get an indoor bike trainer is as soon as you feel the conditions outside are holding you back from riding more.

Whether you get a basic indoor trainer or a smart trainer is a question of budget. If budget isn't an issue and you're wondering if a smart trainer is that much better than an entry-level trainer, I believe the answer is yes.

Training indoors is mind-numbing at the best of times, and you're talking to an expert because I live in Winnipeg where we only get about seven months of outdoor cycling weather a year. I've always found riding indoors on basic trainers while listening to music or watching movies so, so, SO boring. My local friends thought they had it figured out and instead of watching movies they'd ride watching Sufferfest or watching a TrainerRoad workout, but they still complained when they had to do trainer workouts and their consistency plummeted in the winter.

When I first tried Zwift, it was a total game-changer. My first Zwift ride was 70 minutes—on a basic trainer, 70 minutes feels like three weeks. Now, I regularly do three-hour Zwift rides and it doesn't feel like a slog.

I would strongly recommend a smart trainer over a basic trainer; in my experience, the athletes who have smart trainers cycle more often and enjoy their training much more. An approximately $600 bike trainer is all you need; the $1,500 trainers are nice, but they're not a requirement. Look up reviews and recommended bike trainers on the DC Rainmaker website.

I'm going to make a slightly controversial suggestion here: When you get a smart trainer, whether you're using Zwift or another training app, don't exclusively use ERG mode where the smart trainer does the work to keep you at the target pace. One of the ways Zwift keeps you engaged is through the need to shift and adjust your effort in simulation mode. More importantly, though, those small micro-adjustments you need to make to reach target effort levels are something you're going to have to do in a race and they have a positive training effect. Riding at a perfectly steady effort level does not give you that same positive training effect. Finally, riding in ERG mode is based on FTP numbers and, as we indicated earlier, there are days where you'll want to veer slightly from those predetermined power numbers.

CYCLING SHOES vs. TRI SHOES $100 - $400

Although we addressed shoes a little earlier on, you'd be surprised how many questions come up about them.

The differences between road cycling shoes and triathlon cycling shoes are becoming fewer and fewer. Historically, tri shoes were designed to be better ventilated than road cycling shoes so barefoot athletes could dispel the sweat and liquids that fall into the shoes. The way tri shoes opened also allowed them to stay open while clipped into the bike in transition so the athlete could easily slide their foot into the shoe after mounting the bike.

Clipped-in and opened-up tri shoe

Road cycling shoes are becoming quite easy to slip into with the improvements of things like the Boa closure system (the dial that tightens the shoe with a series of wires), and they're becoming quite well ventilated. Road cycling shoes also seem to have a less-bulky closure system. See the pictures of a road cycling shoe and a tri shoe below, to see what I mean:

Road cycling shoe

Tri shoe

Having the ability to easily slide your foot into a triathlon shoe while performing a flying mount coming out of transition is pretty critical if you're in a draft legal Sprint or Olympic triathlon, but for most people, a road cycling shoe will be fine. More and more elite triathletes are using road cycling shoes in the longer distance races because they feel there's an aerodynamic benefit to the smoother profile, and they aren't concerned about the several-second time penalty of having to slide their foot into a road shoe. See the picture below of Patrick Lange in road cycling shoes during the 2018 IRONMAN World Championship bike:

Road cycling shoes will perform just fine if that's what you've got; tri shoes will be a little more comfortable if you're barefoot because they're smoother on the inside and will breathe better.

I don't recommend using mountain bike shoes because they're designed to keep your foot so well planted inside the shoe that they're quite difficult to get on and off, and the time penalty is not insignificant with these shoes. (Not to mention, they're noticeably heavier than road/tri shoes.) If mountain bike shoes are all you've got for your first race, fine, but if you're purchasing your first pair of cycling shoes, go with road or triathlon shoes.

One final note about cycling shoes: there are some posts on the internet saying that triathletes are ridiculous if they don't use mountain bike shoes because they can put them on and run through transition quicker than anyone else. I think these posts are just trying to be contrarian because, first of all, have you ever tried to run in mountain bike shoes?! It's the clunkiest and slipperiest thing you can do! And secondly, triathletes are A-type people who obsess over fractions of a second and typically have the money to buy speed any way possible. If mountain bike shoes really were any faster, all triathletes (particularly at the elite levels) would have caught on to it by now.

LUXURY PURCHASES

SHIMANO 105/SRAM RIVAL vs. ULTEGRA/SRAM FORCE vs. DURA ACE/SRAM RED vs. CAMPAGNOLO

Groupsets (groupos or components) are the system that makes the bike tick: the brakes, the shifters, the drivetrain, and the wiring. The two main manufacturers of groupsets are Shimano and SRAM (I'll wrap up the talk about Campagnolo, or "Campy," by saying that they're great groupsets, but for most triathletes, much too proprietary and an unnecessary upgrade).

Shimano and SRAM each have a hierarchy of good (Shimano 105 and SRAM Rival), better (Shimano Ultegra and SRAM Force), and best (Shimano Dura Ace and SRAM Red). Both manufacturers make excellent groupsets, but there are some small differences to consider between the two.

Shimano groupsets tend to be a little heavier than the comparable SRAM groupsets, but Shimano groupsets are much more common and easier to find parts for. You'll often find a Shimano tent at IRONMAN races, so if something goes wrong with your bike, the odds of being able to get it fixed at the last minute is better if you've got Shimano components. I recommend Shimano components simply for the "Oh crap!" factor that has a high likelihood of happening as you travel to races.

As I mentioned earlier, when it comes to selecting a level of groupset, I recommend Ultegra or Dura Ace for the simple reason that those will be easier to resell. The performance difference between Shimano 105 and Ultegra is significant while the performance difference between Ultegra and Dura Ace is small. Each groupset gets a little lighter as you go up a level, and a little more precise. Dura Ace chains and cassettes, however, will wear more quickly than Ultegra because they're light. I know people who, on their training bike, put Dura Ace everywhere besides the chain and cassette where they use Ultegra. Either selection is fine.

ELECTRONIC SHIFTING

The final thing to consider with groupset selection is electronic shifting versus mechanical shifting. Electronic shifting is the type of shifting you get with a "Shimano Di2" or "SRAM ETap" groupset. Rather than the gearshifts coming as a result of a cable pulling your shifters from one gear to the next, the shifting is done electronically where a signal is sent from the shifters on your handlebars to the front or rear derailleur, which then shifts gears very precisely.

Di2 (Shimano) weighs just a smidge more than mechanical, but the benefit is the precise shifting that Di2 offers. Di2 shifting actually self-tunes so you won't have slight chain rubs or a slightly misaligned chain; if you have a better-tuned chain line, you'll go faster.

The one HUGE drawback to Di2 is that it's quite a bit fussier than mechanical groupsets. Di2 is kind of like a modern car where you need specialized software and training to understand how to troubleshoot and tune-up the groupset, whereas mechanical groupsets are much easier to work on and the learning curve to maintain your bike is fairly easy.

If you're mechanically inclined, have a good relationship with your bike shop, don't mind extra work having to charge, tune and maintain your bike, and you want the best groupset you can buy, then go with Di2. If you want reliability and not having to worry about working on your groupset all the time, then go with mechanical.

TIME TRIAL-STYLE HELMET

A long tail triathlon helmet is slowly becoming an endangered species on the bike course. In the early 2000s, you'd see athletes with helmets featuring a 6-12" long tail coming off the back of their heads; the thought being that you wanted to take up space between the back of your head and the start of your back (less space means less air turbulence, which means more aerodynamic).

There are two problems with these long tail helmets. As we've already discussed, when athletes start looking around while riding, that long tail ends up increasing drag as it flares off to the side or above the rider's head when they look down to grab a drink or look at their bike computer. Second, those long-tailed helmets are heavy and they place stress on the upper body that results in body stiffness when the triathlete gets onto the run.

What's becoming much more common these days is a moderately long tail helmet that's long enough to provide a little more aero advantage than a road cycling helmet, while not being so penalizing as the super long-tailed helmets. An example of this moderately long-tailed helmet is the Lazer Wasp Air Tri that I'm using in the picture below.

Interestingly, I've pressed several companies for the wind tunnel results of their aero-road helmet vs. their longer tail helmet and none of them would release the data. This leads me to believe that the time savings of a longer tail helmet are minimal; if they were enormous, you'd have triathletes all over the world buying both a training helmet AND a long tail race helmet. So, don't stress out about buying a super-aero race helmet.

If you do decide to purchase an aero race helmet and are wondering if you should go with a built-in visor or just wear sunglasses, you can go with either. Cam Wurf has done testing in the wind tunnel that has found no aerodynamic benefit to a visor and no aerodynamic penalty to not having a visor and using sunglasses to shield your eyes instead (he set his first course record in Kona with sunglasses and his second course record with a visor).

Personally, the main reason I like using an aero race helmet with an integrated visor is that they're very quiet. In training, I can hear my music or a podcast much more clearly and will often use my aero helmet for long solo road bike rides so I don't have to hear harsh winds. In racing, it allows me to hear my breath a little better and concentrate on executing my race.

Bottom line: if you want a super-aero race helmet, by all means, get one. Just don't expect it to add as much speed as upgrading from a traditional road helmet to an aero road helmet.

RACE TIRES AND LATEX TUBES

Race tires and tubes are the ultimate luxuries for someone with money burning a hole in their pocket. Upgrading your rubber will save between 2-15 watts on the bike depending upon which tubes and tires you're starting with.

There are several levels of rubber for your bike, and they each have their own ideal use case:

Stock rubber that comes with the bike: Stock tires and tubes are heavy and tend not to be incredibly durable or puncture resistant. This setup is fine for general training if your roads aren't too rough.

Really tough rubber: Something like a Gatorskin is a really tough and puncture-resistant tire that works well if your roads are rough. These types of tires are very slow, and if you ever ride on icy conditions, you'll find they're so stiff, they slip a lot more than most tires. I only recommend these tires if your roads are extremely rough.

All-around tire: These tires are models like the Continental Grand Prix 4000 or the S-Works Turbo. These are the tires I use for my training as they're fast enough that I can still go hard in a group and not feel like I'm fighting my tire as I do with the Gatorskins, but they're puncture resistant enough to withstand a lot of miles.

Race tire level 1: These tires are models like the S-Works Turbo Pro, which last 2-4 races and are only meant to be used on race day. They'll be more puncture resistant so if the roads are rough where you're racing, you might not want to use these. They're a little faster and a little lighter, and should be paired with latex tubes.

Race tire level 2 (cotton tires): These tires are one use only and extremely puncture prone. Unless you're a pro who needs to risk flats in exchange for every advantage you can get, I wouldn't recommend these tires. These tires should also be paired with latex tubes.

Something to consider with your tires is that even Cam Wurf uses Continental 4000 tires and regular tubes for racing because they're less punctureresistant and he wants to minimize the chance of a flat; a flat tire will make your times MUCH slower than the few seconds you might save with faster tires.

Finally, tubeless tires without a tube inside are becoming more and more common with mountain bikes and occasionally road bikes. In cases where the tube is quite heavy, like on a fat bike, tubeless tires make a lot of sense. On a road bike, however, saving weight by removing the tube requires a slightly heavier tire so there's not a big weight or performance advantage. The main advantage of going tubeless would be on a set of wheels meant for training, as tubeless tires get fewer flats.

If you want to compare tires, the best resource for understanding which tires are the fastest and which are the most puncture-resistant, is https://www.bicyclerollingresistance.com, where they compare all of the most common models of rubber.

CARBON CYCLING SHOE INSOLES

Quite often when triathletes end up getting a bike fit, they'll also get prescribed a set of insoles for their cycling shoes. This typically provides a little bit of arch support and stability for the foot so there's better power transferred to the pedals, and maybe even more stability in the legs.

In 2018, a company named Solestar reached out to me and wanted me to try their carbon fiber cycling insoles. I'd already been using a set of $40 cycling insoles in my shoes and didn't think a set of fancy carbon fiber insoles would help much.

I tried the carbon fiber insoles and although I wasn't at a time in my season where my peak power output would be high, I ended up putting out the highest power output in a sprint that I'd done all year. And this improvement wasn't by just a little bit. The power output was 10 percent higher than my previous best over the last nine months.

I've since done a little bit of testing and I've always found that carbon fiber insoles from Solestar with their excellent arch support and the grippy fabric on top, always end up resulting in my highest power output both during sprints and steady-state riding.

When I covered these insoles on my YouTube channel, the comments section went berserk on me and accused me of peddling snake oil. I found that kind of funny because it's common knowledge that many triathletes will spend upward of $15,000 for tiny incremental improvements on their already-good triathlon bikes, but the concept of spending a little over $100 to improve the power that's transferred from your legs into your pedals is snake oil.

I'm not saying carbon fiber cycling insoles are an absolute must. I'm saying if you have a little over $100 and want to try a set of carbon fiber insoles, odds are good that you're going to spend less money and get better results than if you had upgraded to a set of race tires.

TRI SADDLE

Split-nose bike saddles have become common on triathlon bikes. Companies like Adamo and Cobb have created bike saddles where the pointy tip is split into two parts. This saddle is thought to take the pressure off the soft tissue of an athlete's underside and distribute that weight across the bum and onto the tougher sit bones.

"Why not do this for all bike saddles?" you might be asking. Because the triathlon bike position in the aerobars is different from the road biking position; instead of sitting upright and already being on your sit bones, you're leaning forward, which closes the hip angle and forces more pressure onto the soft tissue.

Many people find that a split-nose triathlon saddle is much more comfortable, but many people also find them less comfortable. The bottom line is that saddles are like custom-fitted suits: what works well for one person won't work well for other people.

The best course of action is to develop a relationship with a bike shop that will allow you to try multiple saddles, then try multiple positions with each saddle. Eventually, you'll find a saddle that feels more comfortable than others, but you'll still have to "toughen up" your undercarriage no matter what saddle you choose.

MALE vs. FEMALE SADDLES

Finally, it's a big problem that isn't often talked about but females have more challenges finding comfort in the aero position than men because of their different anatomy.

If you're a female and finding your saddle feels extra "smashy," you can look into female-specific saddles designed to fit a woman's body. Saddle companies like Cobb, ISM, and Selle have good options from what I've been told by a few female triathletes.

GETTING AERO

When most triathletes start thinking about getting aerodynamic through the use of a bike fit, they think there's going to be a magic bullet that allows them to get into some position that allows them to cut through the wind like a knife. Unfortunately, this isn't the case.

Much more important than getting aerodynamic is getting comfortable in the aero position; from that basic level of comfort, triathletes can start making their positions more and more aerodynamic. But if an aero position isn't so unbelievably comfortable and natural that triathletes aren't able to stay in that position for hours and hours on end, it's not actually aerodynamic. It might be an aggressive position, but the constant shifting or getting out of the aero position completely negates the aerodynamics.

What you're going to receive in this section is a guide to get a basic and comfortable aerodynamic position established so you can stay in the position for hours on end. Then, we'll provide guidelines on how you can make that position continually more aerodynamic for months and years.

We're going to address the time trial [aero] position and not the road bike fit position. After all, we are triathletes and the aerodynamic position tends to be a much more extreme position triathletes have trouble with. Road bikes and the road bike position are built for comfort, so they're much easier to dial in than the triathlon aero/time trial position.

One final note: if you've gone through this bike fitting process on your own or with a bike fit consultant, and you've worked through the adaptations to get comfortable in this position that we will move through in the following section, and still after two or three months you're experiencing pain in certain areas, there is something wrong. Either the position on the bike is not optimized for you, it's too aggressive for you, or you have a biomechanical body issue that a physiotherapist might be able to help with.

Let's get you dialed in on your bike!

SADDLE HEIGHT

Correct saddle placement is a very finicky thing that you're going to have to play with. Sometimes just a 1mm or 2mm change is enough to go from pain in the butt to absolute comfort. Here are some guidelines for getting your saddle as close to the right spot as possible:

Start by raising and lowering your seat post so it's high enough that when your leg is fully extended, the heel of your cycling shoe just barely rests on the top of the pedal. Your heel should be gently resting on the top of the pedal, not pressing on it firmly, but you also shouldn't have to reach for it.

The saddle height you've determined from the previous point is roughly the highest seat position you want to have.

To determine the lowest level that you want your saddle positioned in, you can lower it as much as ½ inch from the highest point.

Newer triathletes will tend to want to be closer to the lower limit of saddle height position to take the pressure off of the lower back while more seasoned triathletes tend to be at the higher limit of this position.

Play with the saddle height between these two limits to find a spot that feels comfortable for you.

SADDLE FORE AFT

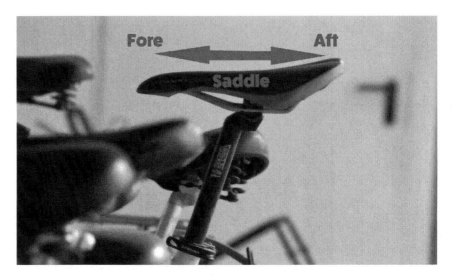

Fore Aft saddle position

Placing the saddle forward and backward in the proper position ["fore" and "aft"] is going to take a little bit of trial and error. You want the saddle as far forward as possible, which will open up the hips to a wider, less scrunchy position while still being in a stable position.

As a starting point, you want the saddle in a position where there's roughly 1 to 2 inches of saddle sticking out behind your butt after you've leaned forward and put your elbows on the arm cups.

Start by positioning the saddle level with the ground [not tilted downward or upward] with the seat post clamp in the middle of the rails underneath the saddle. From this position, start moving the saddle forward in 1mm to 2mm increments until you reach a point where it feels uncomfortable. From this point, move the saddle back just slightly until you get into a very stable position. You'll know when you find it.

Comfort and stability on the saddle are much more important than getting the saddle as far forward as possible so while I say you want the saddle as far forward as possible, a more important thing is to make sure you feel like the saddle is stable underneath your butt.

SADDLE SELECTION

If you've gone through this saddle positioning process and after a few weeks or months of riding in this position you still find you develop pain from riding, the final step you can take is selecting a new saddle at a local bike shop that has access to a saddle pressure mapping system.

A good bike shop will be able to assess your body structure and recommend a short or long saddle, a wide or narrow saddle, and a flat or curved saddle. And if they're really good, they'll even have a device that can be put on your saddle while you ride in the shop and assess if there are any pressure points that might be causing you pain.

Split-nose saddles tend to work well for triathletes because they are designed to work for the position of time trialing with the hips rolled forward.

Women have different saddle considerations than men, based on their anatomy. Cobb Saddles has some female-specific bike saddles that a number of female pro triathletes have told me relieve a lot of saddle pressure unique to female riders.

Unfortunately, there's not another way to select a saddle without trying a bunch. That's why a relationship with a good local bike shop will be helpful.

ELBOW PAD PLACEMENT

Elbow pad placement is one of the most critical but least focused-on aspects of proper bike fitting. Fortunately, it's also one of the easiest to get right.

You want the elbow pads placed just slightly out front from directly underneath your shoulders, but, more importantly, you want the elbow pads positioned in a spot where you feel like you can easily put a lot of your weight on them and let everything else relax.

Elbow pads directly centered under elbows, arms slightly outstretched.

I'm a big fan of the recent trend toward larger elbow pads that have a lot of adjustability, so triathletes can get a big meaty surface area to put their elbows on. If you're able to rest your entire body weight on the elbows and not have it feel like it's pinching your shoulders or forearms, you're going to be able to relax your entire upper body and get off the bike feeling fresh.

One of the more common errors in elbow pad placement is that triathletes place the elbow pads too far forward on their forearms, which then creates leverage between the elbow and the shoulders and tension that you'll pay for when you get onto the run. You want your elbows and the weight of your upper body smack-dab in the middle of the elbow pads.

Depending on your bike, adjusting the elbow pads can happen right on the elbow pads with the different screw holes that are made available. You might have to shorten or lengthen the stem that your bike is set up with, or you can even switch to a larger elbow pad that has more adjustability like the 51 Speedshop elbow pads, for example.

AEROBAR LENGTH

Setting the length of your aerobar extensions is very easy. Most aerobar extensions allow you to slide them in and out to vary the length from the elbow pads to the end of the extensions. You want the end of the aerobar extensions to be in line with your palms so you don't have to curl your hands back to grasp them firmly or reach forward to get a solid grip on the end of the aerobars, thus taking your elbows off the pads.

If you're using clip-on aerobars and you're unable to slide the extensions forward and backward to get the right length, this is okay and part of the trade-off we make using clip-on aerobars instead of a true triathlon bike.

The main thing you need to worry about is that you don't want massive shifts in your elbow position, taking your elbows off of a nice, firmly planted spot on the elbow pads.

ELBOW PAD/STEM HEIGHT

Setting the height of your elbow pads comes from either adjusting the number of spacers under the pads or the stem height on your bike. How high or low your elbow pads end up has been one of the largest things that has changed in triathlon bike positions over the past 20 years.

Historically, the thought was that triathletes needed to get as aerodynamic as possible, at all costs, including at the cost of comfort. The thought was that the lower your upper body could get, the more aerodynamic you'd be and the faster you would be on the bike. While these extremely aggressive positions were uncomfortable and made athletes very stiff for the run, it was a trade-off that nearly all triathletes made.

Fortunately, with more wind tunnel testing and aerodynamic data to study, bike manufacturers and athletes have learned that not only was this historic approach wrong as far as how aerodynamic these aggressive positions actually were, but it made athletes slower over a full race when you considered the negative effect that it had on run times.

When Jan Frodeno first stepped up to the full IRONMAN distance, he had a hard time adjusting to the aero position over the length of a full IRONMAN. A few years into racing long-distance triathlons, Jan switched to Canyon Bikes, which invested a huge amount of money into aerodynamic testing to dial in the bike, the position, and the equipment. What they actually found was that, in Jan's case, he was not only more aerodynamic when they brought his position up higher, but he was more comfortable and it resulted in him being able to unleash blazing fast run times after getting off the bike.

The most common approach bike fitters and athletes take to elbow pad and stem height is to make comfort the priority and aerodynamics secondary. Remember that 80-85 percent of the total aerodynamic drag comes from an athlete's body; if you're not comfortable in the aero position, you're going to be shifting around a lot, potentially taking you out of the aero position and making you slower.

That said, proper stem height or elbow pad height limits the amount of rounding that happens in an athlete's back, which is determined by hip and lower back flexibility. If an athlete is extremely flexible, they're able to have a lower elbow pad position but for most people who are new to the aero position, the elbow pads will have to be placed fairly high to get a nice, flat back.

What you can do to make yourself more aerodynamic over time is gradually lower your stem height or reduce the number of spacers underneath your elbow pads. You can lower the elbow pad height roughly ¼ of an inch every three to four months, going through a process of lowering-adapting-lowering-adapting.

Finally, you should know that the aero position can be lower or higher based on the distance of the race. If you're doing a Sprint race that only lasts 30 to 40 minutes, you can tough that out and still be fresh for the run. But if you're doing an IRONMAN distance, it's going to be hard for your body to stay in a tremendously aggressive position for a long period so you want that elbow pad position to be higher.

ELBOW PAD WIDTH

Just like the desire to be slammed as low as possible, a lot of triathletes want to be as narrow as possible, having their elbows tucked together like the pictures they see of their favorite pros. This is a hard position to get into from the start, but it's something you can certainly work toward more easily than getting as low as those pros get with their aero positions.

I recommend age-group triathletes start with elbow pads placed as wide as possible, with the elbow pads pointed at the spot on the aerobar extensions you'll be holding onto. This will make it easy to adjust to the overall aerodynamic position.

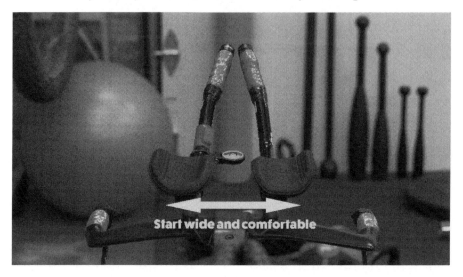

Once you've adjusted to this nice, wide, comfortable position, you can then start bringing the elbow pads in closer together, thus making yourself more aerodynamic and tucking those elbows in. This is a gradual process; as with getting lower, you can move as much as ¼ inch every three to four months.

GETTING MORE AERO

One of the friends I train with is very athletic and naturally flexible, and even in his early 40s, he can crouch down so low that his butt touches his heels.

When he bought his very first triathlon bike, he ended up getting a bike fit from the shop where he bought his bike and the fitter did a flexibility assessment. Upon finding out how flexible my friend was, he proceeded to slam the bike position as low as possible.

My friend was definitely able to get into that position and ride, but the talent he had on his road bike suddenly went away and he could barely put any power into the triathlon bike. He raced the IRONMAN he had been training for and, within just a couple weeks after the race, he ended up having a lower back injury that was so severe, he ended up in a wheelchair for about a half month.

Is the wheelchair related to the bike position? Probably not, but bending over into the aerodynamic position very aggressively without adapting to it can definitely lead to lower back problems. But did the fact he had way less power in the aero position compared to the power that had been able to put out on the road bike, relate to that new, aggressive aero position? Absolutely!

Just because an athlete is flexible and can get into an extreme aerodynamic position doesn't mean that position is going to work well for the athlete. This is why I recommend everyone, no matter what their range of motion might be, start with a fairly moderate aero position. Adapt to that, then make gradual adjustments to get more aerodynamic from there.

Elbow pad with stem height, aero bar extension angle, seat height, really any adjustment to the points of contact that we have with the bike need to be made in small increments. Make adjustments in ⅛ inch to ¼ inch increments every three to four months, and never adjusting more than one or two things at a time.

It might seem like I'm telling you not to worry about aerodynamics. On the contrary, instead what I'm recommending is comfort in the position that allows you to stay in the time-trial position for as long as possible, which is going to be the most aerodynamic effect you'll have over the total duration of the bike. Gradually make that position more and more aerodynamic as you get more comfortable, and in time, you'll slowly look more like the pros you admire.

If you want to save yourself a few hundred dollars and get a basic bike fit done, you can easily do it yourself. At triathlontaren.com/bikefoundations, we've uploaded videos with the four step process we recommend so you can get your bike position dialed in by yourself.

STAYING AERO

Staying aerodynamic is just as important as getting aerodynamic in the first place because 80-85 percent of the aerodynamic drag we have to push through is generated from our bodies, not the bike. But it's not enough to get your bike position super aero, we have to allow you to a) be comfortable enough in that aero position to hold it for hours on end and b) be in a position that isn't so uncomfortable that you're not able to hold power.

In this section, we'll address some of the most common issues that prevent athletes from staying in the aero position and losing huge amounts of time.

BUTT PAIN

The first thing many triathletes experience when they start biking a lot is a sore butt. Don't worry, this gets better. Most of the time when new triathletes start riding a bike, they experience a lot of pain and they believe the solution is to get a big cushioned bike saddle. This is incorrect, and quite often a better saddle is one that has less cushioning! We'll get into that part in a bit.

Pain on your undercarriage from riding a bike is both not as serious as you think, but also potentially more serious. Usually riding more will toughen up your underside. It's kind of a rite of passage for new triathletes. But that doesn't mean you shouldn't take undercarriage discomfort seriously. Some riders who develop saddle sores have allowed them to get so bad that they require surgery to cut them out. Don't let that happen to you!

Your first line of defense to avoid saddle sores is to ALWAYS wear clean bike shorts and to use chamois cream.

When I say clean bicycle shorts, I mean fresh out of the washing machine, clean bicycle shorts. This means every time you finish a ride, you immediately put your bib shorts into the laundry basket to be washed. Using cycling shorts that have sweat and moisture trapped in them creates microscopic bacteria and mold, and when you put them on the next time, it can create an infection on the skin and a saddle sore. This means you might need to buy multiple pairs of cycling shorts; any pair that fits somewhat tightly but comfortably with a nice big chamois will work. Don't feel like you need to spend hundreds of dollars on really high-end cycling shorts. They may look and feel a little better, but the function is the same.

Chamois cream is a disinfectant and lubricating cream that reduces friction; friction can create tiny little cuts on your undercarriage, which can become infected because of sweat and bacteria. Good chamois creams can be used to prevent saddle sores and help cure them once they happen. As far as chamois cream goes, I personally like DZ Nuts chamois cream because it's disinfecting, lubricating, cooling and, for me, has proven time and time again to be the most reliable for preventing saddle sores before they start AND fixing sores once they've occurred.

If you've followed the saddle positioning guidelines from the previous section, kept your bike shorts clean, and use chamois cream every time you ride, but you're still getting pain from your bike seat, it could be caused by an improper position of the bike seat or you might need a new bike seat altogether.

CHAPTER 4

BIKE HANDLING SKILLS

As far as triathletes are concerned, you don't have to worry about becoming the best bike handler in the world. But you do need to be stable enough on your bike so you're not swerving side to side; each swerve side to side, no matter how small, makes the bike course you're racing on longer. We need to develop enough confidence on the bike so that if you were placed on a lane line on a road, you could stay on that lane line without a huge amount of tension in your body.

Most often the reason for the little bits of swerving back and forth is instability in the body caused by lack of confidence and calmness. Proper bike handling for triathlon is really quite easy; all we have to do is ride in a straight line. This is an easy thing to develop and can be done with just a few drills.

If you're riding a road bike, you're going to have an easier time developing good bike handling skills than if you're on a triathlon bike. Triathlon bikes are a lot twitchier, which is one of the reasons why I recommend triathletes start on road bikes. But you're going to need to develop these skills with the aerobars so it's not critical to do this on a road bike or a triathlon bike.

The sequence of drills you're going to follow to develop good bike handling skills, which will allow you to ride in a straight line and make the bike course as short as possible, is listed below:

STEP 1: Set up your bike in a stationary position on a trainer.

STEP 2: Start pedalling while your hands are on the main base bar.

STEP 3: While still pedalling, take one hand off the bar and reach down and touch your foot at the top of the pedal stroke. Repeat this going back and forth with each hand.

STEP 4: As you get more and more confident with this, gradually reach down farther and farther so you can touch your hand at lower and lower points of the pedal stroke.

STEP 5: Now, start doing this drill with your arms starting in the position of the aerobars. Gradually reach down lower and lower.

STEP 6: Now, take this drill outside and, starting with your hands on the base bars, perform this drill while riding slowly on grass. Riding on the grass is safer for you and it's going to cause you to ride more slowly, which is going to force you to focus on your balance and control of the bike.

STEP 7: Now, perform this drill while riding slowly in an empty parking lot.

STEP 8: Gradually increase your speed while riding in the parking lot, and eventually work your way up to riding in the aerobars and being able to reach down and touch your foot while pedalling.

Performing that sequence of drills will develop your bike handling skills much better than most triathletes are capable of doing. You're personally going to be more confident on the bike, and you're going to be shortening the course and riding faster on your bike leg than the triathletes who are riding at the same speed.

You will have developed core stability that allows you to make small adjustments instead of big swerves, which are inefficient and slow you down.

UPPER BODY DISCOMFORT

The next thing that triathletes and cyclists notice when they start riding outside is that their upper back and shoulders start getting sore. Addressing this will come in two phases.

The first phase of addressing upper body soreness just comes from spending more time on a bike. All those little micro-movements to ride straight, brace yourself from the wind, and during turns, takes a toll on the body. We have to develop the muscular endurance to handle those things without getting sore. This takes time for new riders but will get better over a matter of 10 to 12 rides. Even seasoned triathletes will go through this in the spring when they get off the winter trainer and out onto the road again.

The second phase of addressing upper body soreness comes when triathletes start getting onto their aerobars. This is a very unnatural position for our bodies, and we have to adapt to it properly.

The first thing you need to do to alleviate upper body soreness when getting into the aerobars is to get the elbow pads of your aerobars in the right spot. For most new triathletes, this will be the widest setting you can select while still being able to point the elbow cups at the spot on the aerobar where your hands will rest. This is going to stop your shoulders from having to be scrunched, causing tension in your upper back.

The next thing you need to do is ease into the aero position gradually. You want to start spending time in the aero position two to three months out from your race, and even most seasoned triathletes will have to start with as little as three to five minutes at a time, gradually building up a minute or two each week until they're just as comfortable in the aero position as they are on the base bars.

You don't have to spend the entire duration of every single ride on the aerobars all year. This will probably hurt your bike fitness because riding in that aero position makes it hard on your body to put out high levels of power. Instead, a good way to balance maintaining fitness while maintaining comfort in the aero position is to do one ride per week that has a lot of time in the aero position, while the rest of your riding is out of the aero position and focused on harder efforts, general long riding, and fitness building. The best time trialists in the world follow this balance.

LOWER BACK PAIN

The next thing that might get sore when you start riding your bike is your lower back. This is common for a lot of people because most people, myself included, spent too much time every day sitting, which makes our hip flexors tight and puts our glutes to sleep so they can't fire and stabilize our body while we're pedalling.

This lower back pain might get better just by riding more, but if the lower back pain is caused by glutes that are asleep, riding more isn't going to wake them back up and you might always have instability. Don't worry, this can be solved with just a little stretching and some light strength movements that you can even do while watching TV, just to unlock the ability to stay stable in the saddle and get rid of that lower back pain.

Most muscles on the human body have somewhat of a push-pull effect with other muscle groups: the chest pushes while the back pulls, the hips pull the leg forward while the glutes push the leg backward. When imbalances occur, it typically means one of the muscle groups is tight and overdeveloped while the other muscle group has gone to sleep. We fix this by stretching and releasing the tight muscle group and strengthening and firing the sleepy muscle group.

In the case of cyclists with lower back pain caused by tight hips and sleeping glutes from sitting too much, we need to stretch the front of the hips and strengthen the side of the glutes. Perform the following exercises in front of the TV or while doing an activity like answering email, so it's not just more time added on to your day:

1. Stretch the hips with a hip flexor stretch done on both legs, holding the position for two to three minutes per side. While doing this stretch, you want to think about having a flat lower back; a good way to learn how to do this is by doing this stretch inside a doorway, keeping your lower and upper back pressed up flat against the door jam.

2. Strengthen the side glutes [gluteus medius] by doing the following five leg-lift exercises while lying on your side and

placing a hand on your glute med to make sure it's the first muscle that is firing to initiate the leg raise:

- 5-8 leg raises with your toe plantar-flexed (pointed) as your leg is going up and dorsi-flexed (drawn up toward your shin) as your leg is lowering
- 5-8 leg raises with your toe pointed toward the ceiling
- 5-8 leg raises with your toe pointed toward the floor
- 5-8 leg circles counterclockwise
- 5-8 leg circles clockwise

If you do this sequence of exercises three times a week for two to three months, your lower back pain should go away (provided this was the cause in the first place). Not only that, you'll be more stable while you're running and be less susceptible to injury.

CORE STRENGTH

If after all that you're still having lower back pain, upper back pain, feeling unstable on the bike, or if you just want bonus points, you may need/want to strengthen your core. I like the following core strengthening routine because it only needs to be done three times a week, takes only about five to seven minutes, and is totally functional for building strength in all movement patterns.

Perform each exercise in the following routine back to back with no rest in between. Start by doing each movement for 10 seconds and increase in three-second increments as it gets easier to perform until you get to 30 seconds. Once you hit 30 seconds, you can start doing two rounds of this routine where the first round holds each position for 30 seconds and the second round holds each position for 10 seconds (in five years of doing this routine I've never actually gotten past 30 seconds).

- **Exercise 1:** Plank
- **Exercise 2:** Plank with alternating extending left arm, bring left arm back in, extend right arm, bring right arm back in, repeat
- **Exercise 3:** Starting with the right arm plank up-up-down-down pushing yourself into an extended pushup position, then going back down into plank
- **Exercise 4:** Starting with the left arm plank up-up-down-down pushing yourself into an extended pushup position, then going back down into plank
- **Exercise 5:** Side plank
- **Exercise 6:** Side plank on other side
- **Exercise 7:** Side plank on the first side with leg raises
- **Exercise 8:** Side plank on the other side with leg raises
- **Exercise 9:** Side plank on the first side
- **Exercise 10:** Side plank on other side
- **Exercise 11:** V-sit
- **Exercise 12:** V-sit twist and extend done slowly

- **Exercise 13:** V-sit twist and extend done quickly
- **Exercise 14:** Glute bridge
- **Exercise 15:** Glute bridge with one leg extended
- **Exercise 16:** Glute bridge with other leg extended

If you do have discomfort or pain on the bike, you don't need to keep doing these exercises all the time. Doing them on and off throughout the first year or two that you take up triathlon and cycling will develop core stability, body awareness, and muscular firing to the point that you likely won't have to do these regularly for years and years.

Also, if you don't know what these exercises mean, go to triathlontaren.com/BikeFoundations, where I've uploaded a video of this entire Core One routine with the exercises demonstrated and explained word for word.

TO STRETCH OR NOT

A lot of triathletes think that when they get on the bike, because they're very stiff, they need to stretch a lot. They might even go to a bike fit session and the fitter will do a range of motion assessment that, for most people, will say they lack flexibility. This adds to the misguided belief many triathletes have that they need to stretch more.

Mat Steinmetz, bike fitter to a lot of Tour de France riders and the founder of 51 Speedshop, once told me he'd seen some of the best time trialists in the world be so inflexible, they can barely put their heel up on a bench in front of them. Yet, somehow, they can get into an insane aero position on a time trial bike.

What Mat said is that being comfortable and able to put out power in the time trial position, and gradually getting into a more (and more) aerodynamic position isn't about being more flexible, it's about gradual adaptations to the time trial aero position and slowly changing that position over a matter of years until it becomes very aerodynamic.

Tension can be good for endurance sports because it creates an elastic energy return and extreme flexibility can lead to lower performance and injuries. So, we only recommend stretching when there are clear imbalances and not for just general flexibility.

Now that you've got your bike as dialed in as possible within your time and budget, it's time to move on to the training. I realize as I'm writing this, it's actually backward to how I would prioritize approaching anything with triathlon (putting your gear before the training), but the fact of the matter is that people tend to have more questions about what to buy when they start triathlon training than about the training itself.

So now that all those pesky little tidbits are out of the way, let's get onto the important stuff.

CHAPTER 5

OPTIMIZE TWO WORKOUTS A WEEK

JUST TWO WORKOUTS?

Once you've got the bike set up the way you want, now comes the more important part: the training. For developing triathletes, we need to accomplish just two simple things; we need to make sure you can bike for a long period, and we need to make sure you can do so at a slightly hard race effort without fading by the end of the bike leg. Respectively, we will call these two needs endurance and strength.

When most triathletes consider taking up the sport, one of the first things they think is, "How could I exercise for that long?" Endurance is one of the easiest things to build. You'll have absolutely no problem completing the distance.

Over tens of thousands of years, humans survived by hunting and gathering, and staying active on their feet for hours and hours on end. Before weapons were developed, one of the most common ways that humans hunted was called persistence hunting where groups of hunters would run down an animal for hours until the animal fell over from exhaustion. We are built for endurance!

In both 2014 and 2017, when I trained for 27 km and 37 km open-water marathon swims respectively, I spent the first five months of training swimming no more than about 4 km in my long swims. It wasn't until about 10 weeks before the swim that I started increasing my one super long swim each week from 4 km to 6 km and 8 km, eventually building up to just one 15 km swim before the marathon swim. The endurance came on so quickly that it dawned on me how the human body is truly designed to exercise at a low-level aerobic capacity for hours (or sometimes days) on end.

Completing the distance of your chosen race is not going to be your biggest challenge. With some smart training, you will build your aerobic engine to chug along for hours without difficulty. The harder part is the strength component of racing where you don't just need to exercise at a low-level aerobic capacity for a long time, but you need to do so at a challenging race pace. This is where the second requirement of bike training (strength) comes into play.

If you are doing a triathlon completely by yourself and had no time goals whatsoever, with the main goal to be simply just completing the distance, it would be a very easy task. But that isn't what's happening. You're lining up at the start line of a race with adrenaline pumping through your veins and as many as 2000 of your closest friends beside you, all of whom you are competing against. Even though triathletes are really just competing against themselves, come race day we all push a little extra hard because of the environment we're in. Our requirement isn't just to complete the distance at an easy pace, we have to complete the distance at a challenging race effort.

This challenging race effort places a load on the body that is beyond what most of us can do naturally. It's hard enough that it will be difficult to sustain without proper training but not so hard that we can't train for it. This requirement to be able to perform a motion over and over under an elevated intensity for hours on end is called strength endurance, or muscular endurance.

Traditional endurance is built by training our cardiovascular system [our central fitness system], our heart and lungs, and will come on fairly quickly, thus we only have to worry about doing epic long rides and runs for a little while before each race. Strength endurance is built by training the musculoskeletal system [our peripheral fitness system], our arms and legs, and takes longer to build up. So, instead of crushing huge workouts over and over throughout the entire year, most triathletes will do quite well performing shorter workouts that focus on building strength and speed throughout the majority of the year.

You might see pro triathletes crushing big workouts all year round, and it is true they do maintain a very high volume of training all year. But there are some differences between pro triathletes and amateur triathletes that we need to remember:

- Pro triathletes tend to race all year round to maintain an income level to make a living in the sport, whereas amateur triathletes might just have one or two big races a year.
- Pro triathletes need to build up such a huge volume of training that the distances in the race are like a typical training day, but amateur triathletes don't have this level of expectation.
- Pro triathletes' lives revolve around training. They have the time and the life structure to be able to train a huge amount, year-round, which gets offset by a huge amount of recovery. Amateur triathletes have busy lives and don't have the time to recover from huge volumes of training all the time.

So, knowing that, all we need to accomplish is building up a level of endurance to be able to complete our chosen distance at a slightly elevated effort level. How do we prepare for this? Simple stuff, we just build it into our training. All you need to be doing is two workouts each week; one focused on building up the endurance and one focused on building up the strength.

You might be wondering, "Is it really just as easy as doing two workouts a week?" Yes, it is just doing two workouts a week, but that doesn't mean it's easy.

There are no true hacks to triathlon that allow you to train with short and easy workouts and be well prepared for a race. The endurance building workouts are going to have to be appropriately long at some times of the year; it will be physically challenging for you to go that long, and also challenging to fit into your already busy schedule. The strength building workouts, on the other hand, can be short. On Team Trainiac, we have many workouts that are as short as 30 minutes even for IRONMAN athletes, but they're so hard that athletes might be fighting a little bit of puke in the back of their throats.

I hope this doesn't put you off of triathlon, but if you thought that doing a triathlon was going to be easy, would you even enter? The thing to understand about the two-workout bike training system that we're going to recommend is that it isn't about punishing training, workout after workout. It's about having some hard days and some long days at certain points that are just challenging enough to force your body to adapt, in order to be able to go longer and faster. The problem for many triathletes is that they don't go long enough on long days or hard enough on hard days.

With the system of training for the bike that we're going to teach you, all you'll need to do is one intense workout a week and one less intense but longer workout each week.

Finally, it might sound too simple that two workouts a week is enough to make your biking strong enough so that, come race day, you can ride fast and not fade toward the end of the bike.

For the first eight years I was in triathlon, I only biked twice per week and I was able to do a 31-minute 20 km sprint distance bike, a 1:10 40 km Olympic distance bike, and a 2.5hr 90 km half IRONMAN distance bike. When I finally started riding more than just twice per week, the additional rides were either easy bike commutes to and from work, or a very low effort, one-hour recovery ride averaging around 100 watts. The workouts don't have to be immense; they just have to be designed right and that's what we're going to teach you in the upcoming sections.

Before diving too much further into this chapter, you'll need to go to triathlontaren.com/bikefoundations and enter your email address, if you haven't done so already. There will be some calculations discussed in this chapter that you will need to have done for yourself, to apply to your training.

THE ONE-MINUTE WORKOUT

Dr. Martin Gibala, a sports scientist, author of *The One-Minute Workout*, and podcast guest on our show (the Triathlon Taren Podcast), wanted to start researching how short you can make workouts while still getting as much fitness benefit as from traditional, longer workouts. His findings were incredible and provide a lot of tools that I think triathletes underutilize.

In one study, Dr. Gibala found that over 12 weeks, three 20-second bursts done three times per week were just as effective as 150 minutes per week of continuous exercise. Three total minutes of HARD exercise per week generated the same results as 150 minutes of moderate exercise!

In study after study, many researchers found the same thing: on measures of endurance, speed, strength, perceived exertion and pain sensation, intense bursts of extremely hard efforts were just as effective, if not more effective, than long moderate efforts.

In another study, 61 IRONMAN athletes were measured before a race on different physiological factors to determine what athletes should focus on that made the biggest difference in performance. Two things came back as clear differentiators: the ability to use fat as fuel [which we'll discuss in a future book], and the athletes' VO2 Max, which is the ability to consume huge amounts of oxygen while exercising. Improving your VO2 Max is best done with intense bouts of exercise.

"Intense" has a different meaning to everyone. The calculator called Heart Rate Zone Calculator, online here at triathlontaren.com/bikefoundations, will calculate just how hard "hard" should be for you. For the purpose of this training, "intense" means Zones 4 and 5 as calculated in the spreadsheet you should go fill out now.

These findings provide triathletes with a lot of information about how to design their workouts. Knowing that improving VO2 Max provides a huge return on investment, we know that some of our bike workouts are going to have to be very intense. Knowing that intense workouts don't have to be very long, we know we can get a huge amount of benefit from short, intense, really focused workouts. Instead of having to constantly grind out hour after hour on the trainer or out on the roads, taking time away from your family, you can accomplish a lot of fitness gains through workouts as short as just 20 to 40 minutes even if you are training for an IRONMAN.

The benefits of performing HIIT designed workouts are hard to understate: fat loss, better endurance, regulated hormones, better pain tolerance, muscle growth. It's really incredible the multitude of effects one small, really intense workout can have on who you become, not just as an athlete, but as a person.

Before getting into the numerous benefits of HIIT training, we need a quick science lesson: *Hormesis* is a biological phenomenon where a beneficial effect is achieved by exposure to a low-level of stress that, if given in higher doses, would cause harm; the body strengthens itself to defend against the chance that future exposure to that same stress might occur again. Whether or not you support vaccines, the science is the same: you're injected with a small dose of a disease you want to build antibodies against so if in the future you are exposed to that disease, you'll be prepared for it. We can strengthen our body and get a hormetic response in the same way through exercise.

When we exercise hard, it places a lot of stress on the body; stress that could potentially kill us if we were exposed to that hard exertion over and over. So, after a hard workout, to protect itself from the chance of future hard exercises doing damage, a hormetic response happens where the body makes itself stronger, faster, better. The key to initiating this hormetic response is that the stress placed on the body has to be tough, alarmingly tough, to send a signal to the body that danger is coming and you'd better prepare for it.

One of the reasons you see people crossing the finish line of local running races or triathlons who look like your average desk worker and not a superhero who's been trained to withstand constant feats of strength, is that when people train hard, they tend not to train hard enough. People train kind of hard, they feel a little, "Oh, ouch, I'm breathing a bit heavy," and think they're making gains. Yet year after year, people struggle to make progress. Training needs to be one of two things:

➢ Tremendously easy, with workouts getting progressively longer and longer to build your cardiovascular fitness and endurance, or

➢ Bleeding-eyeballs-level difficult, which scares the wits out of your body enough to stimulate improvements.

Getting stronger, faster, better, fitter, and being able to lose weight, play more with your kids, or get across a finish line strong is really quite simple. If you can cycle at 30 km per hour, and do some HARD efforts at 45 km per hour for a while, your body will adapt and get stronger so all of a sudden 30 km per hour will seem pretty easy and you'll be able to cycle progressively faster. Repeat that over and over, always pushing your body to its absolute limit and forcing progress. Pair those hard efforts with good sleep (time to make repairs/gains) and healthy food (raw materials to make the repairs) and you will be a better version of yourself, without question.

Before we get into some of the numerous benefits available to triathletes through HIIT training, it's important to understand that HIIT training is not a panacea; it's not the only thing triathletes should work on in their training. Why, if some HIIT training is good, is not more HIIT training better? A few reasons that it's not:

> ➤ HIIT training is tremendously taxing on the body. Performing intense session after session can result in injury, fatigue, and underperformance.
> ➤ HIIT training is so effective that a little bit goes a long way, so why do more hard work than is necessary? Trust me, when you do the first few HIIT sessions, you won't want to do them all the time.

You need to allow your body to absorb the HIIT sessions in order to get faster. I like to use the phrase stress + rejuvenation = growth (adapted from the book *Peak Performance*, which states, "stress + rest = growth," but I like rejuvenation, because it more broadly describes all aspects of the recovery process like rest, nutrition, and active recovery workouts). If you don't have lighter workouts intermixed with the more intense workouts, you won't be able to absorb those HIIT workouts and reap the benefits of the hard work.

Finally, even though HIIT workouts can improve your endurance, there's no substitute for long workouts. Nothing helps you go long on race day like going long in training. In fact, on Team Trainiac we allow athletes to train for any distance race with as few as four workouts a week. When athletes choose to train just four times a week, we set those four workouts as long endurance workouts because we need to make sure athletes can complete the distance (going really fast doesn't help you in an IRONMAN if you can only do it for a few hours, and run out of endurance before the end).

HIIT is great for a lot of reasons, which we outline below, but it needs to be built into a larger, properly designed training plan that incorporates all aspects of fitness required to get across the finish line strong.

SHORT WORKOUTS IMPROVE STRENGTH AND SPEED

As previously explained, performing HIIT workouts that require you to push harder and go faster than you were previously comfortable going initiates the process of hormesis. As little as 10 to 30 total minutes of hard efforts throughout a week, paired with sleeping at least seven hours a night and good nutrition, will certainly make you stronger and faster; there's almost no way it won't.

Often referred to as VO2 Max (the highest amount of oxygen an athlete can turn into energy each minute), this relates to the top end of intensity that an athlete can produce. This VO2 Max is best improved by really intense workouts. Previous speeds will be easier to reach and peak effort levels will be easier because your muscles can activate quicker, and they'll be stronger.

SHORT WORKOUTS STIMULATE FAT LOSS

Low-intensity training has always been the intensity level associated with fat loss, and it was believed, past 70 percent of maximum heart rate, fat wasn't being burned. It's true, during effort levels above 70 percent of maximum heart rate, fat isn't the primary fuel, but intense exercise stimulates fat burning for 24-48 hours *after* a workout.

The oxygen debt created by HIIT training raises the metabolism and fat burning after a workout, so while you don't burn a lot of fat during the workout, you'll continue to burn fat after the workout is done. Consider the difference between sprinters (HIIT athletes) and marathon runners (relatively slow athletes): sprinters are totally jacked and don't have an ounce of fat on their body, while marathoners can carry a little fat even at elite levels.

Body fat percentage is one of, if not **the most** critical factor, determining how successful a triathlete will be in a race. In study after study, the single factor that unquestionably improves triathlon performance is not training hours, the speed at which you train, or even overall body weight—it's body fat percentage. That means, if we can build muscle and burn fat, we'll be better triathletes.

SHORT WORKOUTS IMPROVE OVERALL HEALTH

Endurance training is hard on the body. It's catabolic in nature, meaning that the more you do it, the more it tears down our muscles. While low-intensity training is easy for our body to handle and recover from, the moderate-intensity, race pace training we have to do occasionally throughout the year breaks down our muscles and can wreak havoc on our hormonal system.

Short intense workouts have a similar effect on the body as lifting weights. Placing a significant load on our musculoskeletal structure through weightlifting, or significantly hard HIIT efforts, causes our body to release anabolic hormones (rebuilding hormones, the opposite of catabolic) to help with the repair process. This anabolic hormone release helps to keep our hormones balanced and reduces the likelihood of overtraining, inability to make progress, sleep disturbances, and adrenal fatigue.

SHORT WORKOUTS IMPROVE PAIN TOLERANCE

Triathlon is going to hurt. Despite making it look effortless on camera, two-time IRONMAN Kona World Champion Patrick Lange once told me that when he came out of the Energy Lab at mile 18 of the marathon during his 2018 record-setting performance, he felt like he was going to blow up and that his eyeballs were bleeding. Whether you're a first-time try-a-tri athlete at a local race or a world champion, you're going to have to suffer if you want to get across that finish line.

Studies have shown that HIIT workouts do a better job than any other workout of increasing an athlete's ability to tolerate discomfort. In fact, VO2 Max only improves roughly 20 percent from a sedentary athlete to that athlete's peak performance VO2 Max, but athletes can still get faster even with the same VO2 Max and thus, the same maximal oxygen uptake, by improving their ability to handle discomfort at the high effort levels.

SHORT WORKOUTS IMPROVE ENDURANCE?!

There are three big buckets, or zones, of training stimuli: low intensity is roughly 70 percent and under your max heart rate, moderate intensity is roughly 70-85 percent of maximum heart rate, and high intensity is above 85 percent of maximum heart rate.

There's nothing like a long, low-intensity ride that's potentially hours longer than you'll be biking in the race, for improving your ability to exercise for hours and hours on end. But, counterintuitively, when compared to moderate-intensity training HIIT training comes out ahead when it comes to improving an athlete's endurance.

Moderate-intensity training, also known as the "gray zone" of training or (as I like to call it) low return on investment training, is too hard to sustain long enough to use for strictly endurance-building workouts. Moderate-intensity workouts also aren't hard enough to cause your body to make any improvements. HIIT training is so hard that your body will produce more mitochondria in the muscles, which means your limbs will be better at utilizing oxygen, so even with the same cardiovascular health and top-end VO2 Max, you'll see improved speed and endurance performance because your muscles can better use the oxygen they receive.

SHORT WORKOUTS IMPROVE MUSCLE RECRUITMENT

Finally, who do you think is going to be able to swim, bike, or run better: an athlete who can access up to 90 percent of their muscle fibers or an athlete who is only able to access 70 percent of their muscle fibers? These numbers are completely fictional, but they illustrate the fact that you want to be able to access as many muscle fibers as possible.

Training at low or even moderate intensities doesn't stress the body enough to force it to "call in all the troops." Pair that lack of muscle recruitment in low and moderate-intensity training with the fact that most of us sit the majority of the day in a position that turns off our glutes and lats, and triathletes who don't force their muscles to work really hard will be operating at less muscle capacity than athletes who have access to more muscle fibers for the same task.

HOW TO PERFORM YOUR INTENSE BIKE WORKOUTS FOR MAXIMUM BENEFIT

Most triathletes find that their time is quite limited during the week so workouts have to be short, but that doesn't mean the workouts have to be less effective. Workouts as short as 20-50 minutes, even for IRONMAN athletes, can be quite effective when done right. The busier weekdays are the days that most triathletes will perform their HIIT workouts because, while properly performed HIIT workouts will improve your endurance, these workouts are not a substitute for the long ride that typically needs to be done during the weekend due to time constraints (of course, substitute the word "weekend" for "days off" if you're a shift worker).

The mechanism for the effect that triathletes receive from HIIT workouts seems to come from two sources: the rapid change from an easy effort to a hard effort, and reaching the super high efforts during those hard efforts. The second source of improvement, really high levels of exertion during the hard efforts, means that you need to be physically quite prepared for the HIIT workout. This means you need to address your nutrition and your recovery leading into the workout properly.

Even if you're practicing a lower-carb approach to triathlon training (which we'll address at length in another book or course) you'll want to take in 30-40g of carbohydrates in the 60-90 minutes before a HIIT workout. This will allow you to top up your muscle glycogen before the workout instead of trying to nail super hard efforts with an empty tank. Related to that, you should not be coming into a HIIT workout fasted. Again, I'll address this in-depth in another resource, but in addition to playing Russian roulette with your hormones, you simply will not be able to exert as much effort if you are coming into a hard ride without carbs or food at all. There is a time and a place for fasted or low-carb workouts and HIIT workouts are not one of them.

Finally, you want to perform these HIIT workouts on days when you're ready. Not only do you need to hit super high levels of exertion that you've potentially never reached before to get the most benefit out of HIIT, but HIIT is taxing on the body and your body needs to be prepared to recover from the hard workout, to absorb the hard work.

To get the most out of HIIT, you want to first try to structure your week in such a way that you don't have a HIIT workout planned immediately after a really hard day of training that will leave you with tired legs (e.g., scheduling a Tuesday night track run followed immediately by a Wednesday morning HIIT workout). Instead, try to have at least 24 or 36 hours between hard efforts.

If you have flexibility in your schedule, you also may want to dose your HIIT training at certain times when you know your body is ready for it. You can use a workout journal and, each day, write down your subjective level of motivation, body soreness, how the workouts the day before went, and how your sleep was. If you notice a trend that your motivation level is low, your workouts didn't feel great, you got less than seven hours of sleep, or your body is sore, you may want to postpone the HIIT workout to a later day when you can perform better.

Bonus points: you can use something like an OURA Ring or the HRV4Training iPhone app combined with the free tracking spreadsheet that you can download from my website here at https://triathlontaren.com/bikefoundations/, to start dialing in the days when you're ready for a hard effort versus the days when you're not.

That's it, half the key to training to nail the bike is setting aside 20-50 minutes just one time a week where you perform a workout that has some sections where you need to turn yourself inside out. It's not like you even have to perform hard for the entire 20-50 minutes, you just need to show up and mentally commit that, when a workout says "HARD 90sec", you give your absolute best for those 90 seconds. These short workouts will make a huge difference in your bike performance, your overall health, and your confidence as a total athlete. Don't hold back, you'll surprise yourself with what you're capable of during the workouts and that will result in surprising yourself come race day.

A listing of twelve sample HIIT workouts from our Team Trainiac website can be found in Chapter 10, later in the book.

CHAPTER 6

THE LONG RIDE

When triathletes get into the sport and struggle through their first several races, it's often because they're not training hard enough or long enough.

We accomplished the "hard enough" in the previous section with the once per week HIIT ride that will improve your speed, strength, muscular endurance, overall endurance, hormones, and body fat percentage. But when it comes to going long and focusing on building your endurance, how long is long enough? And how often do you need to go long? Do you need to perform the nine-hour days that occasionally pop up on Instagram or do you need to complete a mock IRONMAN to complete your actual race? Or besides the short HIIT workout, do all workouts need to take you away from your family and work for hours each day?

Fortunately, the answer to all these questions is that building your long endurance capabilities takes much less time than you think. Just one long ride per week, done at a low intensity, that starts off quite short and ramps up to be fairly long in the final few months before a race, is all you need to build your endurance, not just for the bike but for the entire triathlon.

One thing to note about the long ride that a lot of triathletes overlook is that the long ride is the key tool in our toolbox to help build the body's ability to make it through the entire race. New triathletes often look at each discipline of swim/bike/run individually and think that if they can swim the distance of their race, and bike the distance of their race, and run the distance of their race that they'll able to swim/bike/run each distance on race day. But we're not swimmers who then go for a ride, then go for a run; we're triathletes and we're swim/bike/runners. We need to build endurance to complete all the distances together in just one day. This is hard to do with just swimming or running, but easy to do with cycling.

Pure exercise endurance is the ability for the body to perform for hours on end, and we need to build up the ability to chug along through our training. Let's say you're planning on doing a six-hour half-IRONMAN (70.3) consisting of a 45-minute swim, a three-hour bike, and a 2:15 run. Unless you like wrinkled hands and feet, it's going to be hard to build up six-hours of endurance by swimming for two, three, or four hours.

Running for two to four hours is hard on the body and can lead to injury, so we can't rely on running to build up massive amounts of endurance. But, even though it's significantly longer than you'll be biking on race day, you can easily and quite enjoyably go for a 4.5-hour bike ride, building up endurance for the bike portion of a race as well as the other two sports in the process.

This ultra-long bike ride is what's called the "over-distance" ride, where you ride longer than you'll be riding in the race in order to turn the distance of the bike leg into a cakewalk, and build the capability to exercise for the entire length of a race. Let's get into the specifics of how to do this once a week long-ride.

HOW DO YOU BUILD UP THE ABILITY TO GO LONG?

Your ability to go long is much, much, MUCH greater than you think it is. Humans evolved to run for literally days on end at low levels of effort. Just think about people who complete deca-triathlons (to a cumulative distance of 10 IRONMAN-distance triathlons), or athletes who run 240-mile races, or rowers who row 16 hours a day for months on end to cross oceans. When you look at the resume of many of these athletes, you won't see Olympic-level, sport-specific athletes, you'll see a lot of average people who just gradually built-up the ability to go for hours and days on end gradually, one mile at a time.

At the time of writing this, I've completed two open water marathon swims of 27 and 37 kilometers nonstop (other than treading water for a 60-second nutrition stop at the support boat every 30 minutes.) You might think I did enormous swims for months and months leading up to these events, but you'd be wrong. All I did for both of these marathon swims was four swims a week of 60-90 minutes for six months to build up the strength to swim a long time, then, in the final three months before the long swim, I made one swim per week gradually longer and longer, starting at 90 minutes, eventually building up to a 4.5hr swim done three weeks out from the marathon swim. Altogether, to build up the ability to swim for up to 10 hours, I may have completed just a dozen swim workouts that were longer than 90 minutes.

This same approach is what you can take toward the long bike. Throughout the majority of the year, the "long" bike can be relatively short. Then, in the final 3-4 months before the event, sequentially increase the distance and duration of the long ride 7-10 percent week by week, take a rest week, then pick up the pattern again.

See an example for a 70.3 preparation below:

- **Week 1:** 50 km

- **Week 2:** 55 km (10 percent longer than the previous week)
- **Week 3**: 30 km rest week (roughly 60 percent of the previous week)
- **Week 4:** 61 km (10 percent longer than where you left off)
- **Week 5**: 67 km
- **Week 6:** 40 km rest week
- **Week 7:** 74 km
- **Week 8:** 82 km
- **Week 9:** 50 km rest week
- **Week 10:** 91 km
- **Week 11:** 100 km
- **Week 12:** 60 km rest week
- **Week 13:** 110 km
- **Week 14:** 120 km
- Taper for the race

You'll be amazed how quickly your body progresses from that first ride and soaks up the endurance week by week. By the final rides, you might find the longest ride of the year feels easier than the first ride of the year. Like I say, you're built to become an endurance machine so with the proper endurance build, paired with sleep and nutrition, you'll be riding for hours without difficulty in no time.

HOW OFTEN DO YOU NEED TO RIDE LONG?

Just like we don't have to perform brutal HIIT workouts day in and day out, we also don't have to ride long all the time. Just one long ride per week is more than enough to build a massive amount of endurance.

There are a huge number of things triathletes need to develop the capabilities for: leg strength for hills, the ability to bike after swimming, the ability to run after biking, the ability to push harder and spike the heart rate then to calm back down without blowing up, and on and on. But it's important to remember you don't have to train for all of these requirements every workout, so we bike hard on some days and bike long on other days, creating the ability to do both on race day. Endurance and the ability to go long is critical, so we dedicate one workout each week to swimming long, one to biking long, and one to running long (FYI: swimming and running long are treated differently than biking as they don't require the ultra-long training day).

HOW LONG IS LONG ENOUGH?

This is where the concept of the "over-distance" workout comes into your training. Eventually, you want to build up to the point that the bike distance you'll be completing in the race seems tiny, minuscule, and almost just a warm-up for the run. Below are guidelines of how long you'll want to build up to the 7-10 percent increments outlined above:

> **Sprint**: 35-40 km
> **Olympic**: 60-70 km
> **70.3**: 110-130 km
> **IRONMAN**: 5.5 hrs

*There is some benefit to building up your long IRONMAN bike training days to the 200 km rides you'll see pros doing online, but this is unnecessary for amateurs. My belief and experience is that the body's energy systems work in such a way that the body throws a little hissy fit around the 75-90 minute mark, again at the three-hour mark, and around the 5.5-hour mark. Once you're trained to go beyond 5.5 hours, you've reached a point where your body can chug-a-chug along for days on end. So, pair a 5.5-hour ride with a 30-minute brick run and you'll have built up all the endurance you'll ever need.

HOW EARLY DO YOU NEED TO START GOING LONG?

This question is best answered by considering where you're starting from.

We've built a calculator on our website that you can easily find by Googling "Triathlon Taren Training Plan." This calculator generates a very basic training plan that includes the long run and long ride distances for each week based on how far away your race is. These are "dumb" distances because they just build 10 percent each week (intermixed with a rest week every third week.) Would they get you across the finish line for a race? Yes, but they're not ideal because they don't build a foundation of fitness. This approach is kind of like the minimum required training distance. Let me explain a better approach.

If you want to not just get across the finish line, but you want to get across your finish line feeling strong, and perhaps even make progress from previous races you've done, you'll want a different approach than just building 10 percent distance week after week until you achieve one ride of the prescribed over-distances listed above.

Remember that with your training, we want to accomplish two things. We want you to be able to have the endurance for the distance of your race, and we want you to complete the distance at a race pace effort. With those two requirements in mind, working our way backward from the date of your race, I recommend the following approach, which is what we use on TeamTrainiac.com and in my personal training. Here's that approach:

Your taper for a Sprint, Olympic, or 70.3 race should be one week, taper for an IRONMAN should be two weeks.

Your final over-distance ride should be 8-10 days from the date of your race for a Sprint, Olympic, or 70.3, and 15-17 days from the date of an IRONMAN.

In the final eight weeks before your race, you should aim to complete the prescribed over-distance ride followed by a brick run on four occasions.

This is going to turn the distance of the bike leg in your race into such an easy task that we will easily accomplish building the required endurance for your race.

During the final 12 weeks before your race, you want to start including a larger and larger portion (usually toward the end of the ride) of the long ride, which is performed at, or just slightly above, your desired race effort.

This is going to teach your body to function at a high effort level for a long period, accomplishing the second requirement of being able to hold race effort for a period of time.

Prior to 12 weeks out from the race, you'll build up in 10 percent week by week increments.

During your Off-Season and Base Building season, maintain a high enough level of fitness so that it's easy for you to start building up endurance in the Strength and Speed building (also known as Pre-Season) phase of training.

Without an exact example of how to do this build, it might be hard to visualize. Here's an example for a 70.3 build-up of the different sections of training following the guidelines from above.

- **Off-Season and Base Building Season:** Weekly long ride of 1-2 hours at a very easy pace
- **19 Weeks out**: 48 km ride
- **18 Weeks out:** 54 km ride
- **17 Weeks out (rest week):** 32 km ride
- **16 Weeks out:** 60 km ride
- **15 Weeks out:** 66 km ride
- **14 Weeks out (rest week)**: 40 km ride
- **13 Weeks out:** 73 km ride
- **12 Weeks out:** 81 km ride

*At 12 weeks out from your race, start including a portion of the ride at, or just slightly above, race effort starting with five percent of the ride, then 10 percent, then 15 percent (include this portion toward the end of the ride).

- **11 Weeks out (rest week**): 50 km ride
- **10 Weeks out**: 90 km ride
- **9 Weeks out**: 100 km ride
- **During the final 7-8 weeks from the race:** Perform three rides of 110-130 km, 25-30 percent of which is at, or just slightly above, the race effort (remainder of the ride is at an easy Zone 2 pace)

- **8 Days out from race:** Over-distance ride of 110 km, 30 percent of which is at, or just slightly above, race pace (remainder of ride is at an easy Zone 2 pace)
- **Final 7 days before race:** Taper

This approach will give you all the endurance you need, and it will prepare your legs to pedal for a long period even at a race effort. You'll learn how to pace the bike portion of your race, you'll learn how to run after a tiring bike, and you'll be extremely well-prepared for your race. With this approach, you'll certainly be able to get across the finish line strong.

Also, notice that even for a half-IRONMAN, we're not performing week after week of crushing long rides, taking time away from family and work. The vast majority of the season is spent keeping a basic level of fitness, then in the final few months before your race, we start building up a little bit each week. Remember that this is just one long workout each week, the rest of your workouts (besides the long run) can be really effective in under an hour. The total volume of training hours doesn't result in good race performances, but the composition and structure of training hours do result in good race performances (many studies support this).

This is the exact method we use on Team Trainiac, and athlete after athlete is reporting personal bests while feeling less tired and having more spare time throughout the week. The quality and structure of training is much more important than the quantity of training.

HOW HARD SHOULD THE LONG RIDE BE?

While I just had to be the bad guy and let you know that, yes, if you want to get across the finish line strong you will have to perform some long rides, this is the section of the book with some good news: those long rides will be some of the easiest training you'll do all week!

Throughout the vast majority of the year, right up until 12 weeks out from your race, the long ride can be done at an easy Zone 2 pace. This is an easy conversational pace, somewhere under 75 percent of your maximum heart rate, around 60 percent of FTP if you're using power, or around a 4/5 out of 10 levels of difficulty as a rate of perceived exertion. (FTP is your Functional Threshold Power, which is the max power you could theoretically hold for 60 minutes.) This is a very enjoyable pace during which you can easily listen to a podcast or audiobook, enjoy the scenery around you, or for the ultimate cool guy/gal points, go for a social ride with a group of friends.

Going this easy is going to keep you out of the low return on investment training zone that will beat you down without much payback. You'll be burning fat during the ride and really improving your cardiovascular fitness. Training this easy will also keep your motivation levels high because you'll end the workouts feeling fresh, and it will set you up to perform well in the harder workouts during the coming week. You'll polarize your training by going easy and long when you need to go easy and long, and you'll go hard only on the days when you need to go hard, allowing each workout to do a great job at its intended outcome.

This long ride workout only needs to start including some amounts of race effort in the final 12 weeks before your race. As outlined above, you can start by including just five percent of the total ride, somewhere at the end of the ride, at or just slightly above race effort and gradually build up this race effort portion of the ride from there.

What is "race effort" is probably your next question? I intentionally leave "race effort" vague in Team Trainiac training plans because I want athletes to feel out what a sustainable pace is for them developing the tool of body awareness, which will become extremely useful on race day. If all you know is a target race effort heart rate, or power, it will lead to under-performance in your race.

Take, for instance, the athlete who trains off target-power in an average climate, then goes to race in a hot weather climate. There's a good chance that average power might actually be too difficult in hot weather, causing the athlete to blow up toward the end of the bike or on the run.

Or consider an athlete who trains for a certain strict power number, but in the weeks leading up to a race, absolutely nails the taper process and gets a ton of good sleep. In that case, the athlete may artificially hold himself back from achieving a power that he's capable of. A lot of professional triathletes will train with power, and race with a power meter on their bike, but they'll cover up the bike computer with tape so they don't see a high power number and freak out.

Here are some guidelines for what "race effort" should feel like on a rate of perceived exertion scale out of 10.

- ➢ **Sprint**: 8/10
- ➢ **Olympic**: 7/10
- ➢ **70.3**: 6-7/10
- ➢ **IRONMAN**: 6/10

The best way to know your race effort will be to perform long rides that include a chunk at the end that is "race effort," then go for a run immediately after the bike. If you cramp or fade drastically during the brick run workout, you likely paced your race effort during the bike too hard and you'll have to dial it back. If you find that the run is very easy, then bump up the race effort a bit during the next workout. Keep performing this in multiple workouts until you get a sense of an effort level that is sustainable, then look at your heart rate monitor and power numbers during these race effort, sweet-spot workouts, and use that data as a guideline for what your pacing should be on race day.

Perform these long, easy rides once per week, and gradually build up until you can perform several over-distance rides in the few months before your race. Include some efforts at race pace and you'll be well-prepared for whatever race you choose!

If you're wondering exactly how long you should be riding right now, or at any point in the course of your training season, go to the spreadsheet called Triathlon Training Plan Calculator at triathlontaren.com/bikefoundations. There, you can enter the date of your race and the number of workouts you want to do each week, and you'll get a template training plan based on what we recommend for our TeamTrainiac.com athletes.

OPTIONAL BONUS RIDES

The two-ride system that I've just laid out for you is more than enough to become a very talented rider. Provided you do the hard rides REALLY hard, and the long rides really easy but progressively longer and longer, you're consistent, and you rejuvenate your body with more than seven hours of sleep a night and eat good foods, you will get faster! There's no way around that.

That said, sometimes athletes wonder if just two workouts per week in each discipline is enough. For biking, I'd say that the answer is yes but if you have additional time and the desire to drastically improve your bike skills, you can add bonus workouts throughout the week. IRONMAN Kona bike course record holder Cam Wurf calls these "general rides." He uses them just to keep the legs familiar with the pedal stroke, facilitate recovery, and build up even a little bit more leg muscle durability.

DISCLAIMER: *This book is written for developing triathletes and the "typical" age grouper. If you're looking at topping the podium in large IRONMAN branded races or qualifying for a world championship, you may very well have to add a third very challenging ride each week. For the average weekend warrior who wants to be well-prepared but not have it be at the expense of their family life and work commitments, two well-designed rides are more than enough. In 2017-18, I qualified for the 70.3 World Championship, finished third overall in a local Olympic distance tri, and PB'd in back-to-back races going 4:41 and 4:36, all on just one long ride a week of 2.5-4 hours, one hard ride a week of 45-75 minutes, and one 60 minute very easy (100w average) recovery ride per week.*

A "general ride" is a ride that isn't focused on making you faster or able to ride farther. Instead, the general ride is a low-intensity ride that gets the blood moving to facilitate recovery, in order to absorb the harder or longer sessions done elsewhere in the week. This ride also increases weekly mileage so that your legs continue to do what Gwen Jorgensen refers to as "callousing" (essentially just hardening the eff up!).

This ride is entirely optional. An additional one general ride throughout the week will certainly provide benefit to your biking skills, two additional general rides throughout the week will have also benefit but that second general ride won't be nearly as beneficial as the first, and if you start getting into three or more general rides per week, you're getting into severely diminishing returns and likely taking time away from swimming and running, or even family and work.

Here are some guidelines for how to structure the optional third, fourth, or dare I say, fifth bike workout in a week:

➢ Keep the intensity very low: under 70 percent of max heart rate and under 50 percent of FTP (if using power)

➢ The ride length should short enough that you don't feel fatigued after it, but long enough that it feels like there's a purpose for doing it. For some athletes this means thirty minutes, others can ride up to two or three hours at an easy pace and not feel fatigued. This is up to you to determine.

➢ If you want to make this ride more purposeful, you can include some one-legged pedalling or some low cadence over-gear work (we'll discuss this in more detail in the Muscular Endurance section of the book).

> ➤ Use this time to catch up on podcasts, ride with friends—anything that allows you to save some time elsewhere in life.

> ➤ This ride can easily be your daily commute to work by bike. Just realize, however, even though commuting to work by bike is typically done at a very low intensity, it may still provide enough of a training stimulus that it impairs your other swimming and running workouts. You can't just slap commuting by bike on top of a training plan without accounting for it.

The two rides per week system is a great place to start when you take up triathlon. You'll get across any finish line strong and walk up to your start line well-prepared. As you progress in the sport, you might want to revisit the idea of a third or even a fourth ride each week because of our three sports, cycle training is more strongly correlated with faster overall times (in most studies, it edges out running just slightly, but beats swimming by a wide margin).

Cycling is also very low impact, so it can be done frequently without impairing the other sports or leading to injury. And most importantly: BIKES ARE FUN! So, once you feel you've got a handle on scheduling training using the two rides per week system, I'd recommend coming back and considering this chapter again.

CHAPTER 7

OPTIMIZE YOUR STRENGTH

GET THE MOST OUT OF YOUR RIDE

If you ever decide to go down the National Center for Biotechnology Information (NCBI) research rabbit hole with regard to triathlon, you'll find that studies generate mixed results when it comes to whether training volume (total amount of hours spent training each week) makes a big difference in overall triathlon performance.

Some studies say that more is better and that you need to accumulate massive hours of training to be successful. It makes sense because that's what pros do, right? But other studies say that training hours don't predict or even contribute to overall triathlon performance. Then we interview PhD-level sports scientists and elite-level triathlon coaches like Paul Laursen, who say that if done well, a 15-hour training week can be as effective as a 25-hour training week.

When I started diving into these studies, I had a hard time figuring out what was actually right, but after many weeks down the research rabbit hole and after speaking with many well-qualified coaches, what's become clear is that not all training hours are created equal. Instead of accumulating training hours blindly, what's more important is the *composition* of the training hours that you put in. We need to make sure that the work we're putting in is effective (the two ride a week system does this) and we aren't just mindlessly training away with little return on the time spent suffering.

The same approach needs to be taken with the strategy we use to make sure the two rides a week system allows you to show off that awesome work you've put in. You might be incredibly fit, but if you show up to a race and ride the first half of the bike like a demon, you're probably going to have a bad rest of your day. Or if you've done all your riding on the trainer or flat roads and don't know how to tackle hills and wind, you're probably going to have a bad day. Or if you've done your training properly but paid no attention to shifting and gear selection, you're going to be putting a lot of that fitness out the side of the bike chain and not into moving forward.

The composition of your training is just as important as doing the training itself.

In this section, we're going to teach you some of the methods you can use to get the most out of your time spent training and the most out of the fitness you've built, come race day. The strategies outlined in the next chapter are ways to either a) bike faster with the same effort or b) get more out of the same training workloads. Free speed, Trainiac!

CHAPTER 8

HIGH-RETURN CYCLING

POLARIZE AND PERIODIZE YOUR TRAINING

Regardless of what race you do, your race effort and race distance can be described as "moderately long and moderately fast," which is a very gray zone training effort that doesn't generate a huge fitness improvement but takes a lot out of your body.

Training throughout a season evolves and changes a lot. The process of creating a training plan, a training week, and modifying the different aspects of training that change throughout the year is the topic for another entire book or guide (take a look at triathlontaren.com as it might be out by the time you read this), but we'll touch on some basic points now.

During the off-season, which is typically 6-10 weeks long, workouts need to be only as long as you feel like doing and with very minimal difficulty. These workouts can be as short as 15-20-minute swims or 30-minute bikes. Try not to end workouts feeling tired, as this is a time for your body to repair itself from the previous season.

Next comes the base-building phase where workouts become longer and more regular; this will now look like a regular training plan with scheduled workouts at specific times throughout the week. Workouts don't need to be long just yet, but they should be long enough that you're a little challenged by them. HIIT workouts also start getting introduced with short bursts of intensity and lots of rest in between.

Strength and Speed Building Season comes next (some coaches call this pre-season) and this is where the hard work really starts. Long workouts start becoming progressively longer and longer while maintaining low-intensity to make them manageable. HIIT workouts become more challenging by increasing the number of hard efforts in workouts, or reducing the rest time between intervals, or increasing the length of time of the hard efforts.

Race season is last, and this is where your training will start to closely resemble a race. Long rides will remain long, but a longer portion of that long ride will be done at race effort instead of a low-intensity. HIIT workouts will also have reduced intensity but longer durations of the intense sections and shorter rest periods. You'll be taking the great base of endurance and speed you built during the previous seasons, and you'll be sharpening your fitness so your race distance and intensity feel like a breeze.

What's the right amount of low-intensity (60-75 percent of maximum heart rate) vs moderate-intensity (75-85 percent of maximum heart rate) vs high-intensity (more than 85 percent of maximum heart rate) training that you should aim for over the course of a season? There's no magic bullet number but the general guideline is that throughout an entire season, you should aim for the following breakdown, which you can find in whatever training app you're using (Garmin Connect, Training Peaks, Today's Plan, Strava):

➢ **70-80 percent low-intensity**: You'll do almost 100 percent low-intensity during the off-season and base building season. As you get closer to your races, the proportion of your weekly training that is low-intensity will decrease and moderate-intensity will increase.

➢ **5-15 percent moderate-intensity:** This is the low return training zone so you don't want to spend too much time in this zone. You'll spend almost no time in this zone during the off-season or base building season, then as you progress into the strength and speed building season and as your race gets close, you'll spend larger and larger amounts of time in this zone.

➢ **10-20 percent high-intensity:** High-intensity training will be utilized in every training season besides the off-season, where you'll be focused solely on low-intensity.

As I mentioned earlier, the topic of creating an annual training plan, a training week, and training seasons is a large topic that I'll address in another book or guide, which you can look for on triathlontaren.com, but it's already all automated for athletes on TeamTrainiac.com. The key takeaway that you need to understand at this point is that you should try to avoid the moderate training intensity because it's low return and high cost on the body. Instead, focus primarily on long and easy or short and intense right up until closer to race season, where you'll start introducing more and more moderate-intensity training efforts to dial in your race pace.

Following this polarized training method is automated for our athletes on TeamTrainiac.com and it is what will allow you to build massive amounts of endurance and speed without feeling like you're pounding yourself into the ground, day in and day out.

END OF RANGE EFFORTS

Very much related to polarized training is the concept of "end of range training." One thing a lot of triathletes make a mistake about is, they don't train significantly close enough to the end of their range; instead, they train in ways that are within their current capabilities. End of range training can mean several things:

- Training extremely high cadences or low cadences.
- Training extremely high-power numbers or low-power numbers.
- Polarizing your training with either VERY easy biking or VERY hard biking.

A very broad statement I can make about your training is that you should let each workout be well-designed for its intended purpose and that you should largely avoid training in the "low return zone" until very close to your race. This low return zone is approximately 75-85 percent of your maximum heart rate.

With most aspects of training variables that you'll be manipulating throughout a season, you'll want to build up toward the end of your range. For example, in our How to Swim course on ProTriathlonTraining.com with Lucy Charles-Barclay and Reece Barclay, they explained that one way to increase stroke rate (number of strokes per minute) is to try to swim lengths of the pool at almost DOUBLE your current stroke rate. Performing such an exaggerated drill will force your body to adapt and overcompensate very quickly, and you'll be able to make rapid improvements.

When you want to make improvements to your capabilities in triathlon, keep this principle of "end of range training" in mind and incorporate it. Don't go from zero to 100 when you start using end of range training. First introduce the new exaggerated technique or movement gradually for a few weeks to adapt, then include small bursts of extremely exaggerated end of range training, gradually increasing the duration as it becomes more and more comfortable.

CADENCE OVER GEAR & HIGH CADENCE WORK

Cadence is the revolutions per minute that occur while you're pedalling. Typical cadence falls between 80-100 with optimal race cadence usually between 85-95.

Cadence higher than 95 tends to be inefficient because it leads to bounding around on the bike, shooting your heart rate up quite high and burning through a lot of fuel, which we want to avoid in a race. Low cadence, under 85, feels good for a lot of cyclists and results in a lower heart rate and slower usage of fuel, but it tends to break down muscle fibers more quickly, which can lead to a bad run.

While extremely high and low cadences for extended periods of time should be avoided during your race, there will definitely be times when you don't have a choice. Go up a hill and your cadence is naturally going to drop, shift some gears or go down the backside of a hill and your cadence will spike. We want to train your legs to handle these changes in cadence so that when it occurs during a race, it doesn't take a lot out of your legs.

High-cadence training should happen in short bursts because there are rare times that we have to ride at super high cadences in races. We can always shift into a higher gear fairly quickly so spikes in cadence are short. During the season it's good to include efforts at higher cadences building toward our end of range gradually starting with 30 seconds at 100rpm with low-intensity, eventually progressing toward two minutes at +110rpm with moderately high intensity.

Low-cadence cycling, on the other hand, is one of the most powerful training methods you can use; it's something more and more coaches around the world are incorporating, and it's something we use extensively on TeamTrainiac.com. Low-cadence cycling is so powerful because it's, well, powerful. Cycling at less than 85rpm is like a strength workout for your legs. It builds muscular endurance so you can keep riding strong to the end of the bike portion of your race, it occurs at a lower heart rate so you can train at higher effort levels with less stress on the body, it helps uphill riding and into the wind riding strategies, it recruits more muscle fibers, and it creates a more even pedal stroke because you're forced to put effort through the entire revolution.

Low-cadence work can be included in any workout you do, however, low-cadence riding places a lot of torque on the body structure so start including low-cadence work very gradually for 1-2 minutes at a time at a low intensity with just a slightly lower cadence than normal (75-85 for example). As you progress each week, gradually build up the duration and intensity of the low gear work, and lower your cadence.

For example, if your race is in June you may start including low gear work in December with just one minute at low intensity with 70-80 cadence. By February you might be at 5-7 minutes at 65-75 cadence with moderate intensity, and by race season you might be able to perform up to 30 minutes at 55-65 cadence, at or even above race intensity. The key is to build up gradually; you wouldn't try to squat 300 pounds the first time you stepped into a gym, and low-cadence strength work isn't much different so you'll want to ease into it.

This mixture of high-cadence riding and low-cadence riding will build leg strength and resilience to changes in the race conditions. You'll get to the race and be able to hold race efforts for long periods, and your legs will be fresh for the run.

Finally, when it comes to figuring out your unique race cadence, you'll want to look at what you tend to ride during the sections of your workouts that are at race effort. Whatever your average cadence is during those sections is roughly your ideal race cadence. The low rpm training will have the positive effect of lowering your comfortable race cadence and heart rate, which is good, but more is not better because low-cadence cycling creates muscle damage so don't try to artificially lower your cadence.

BIKE MAINTENANCE

You don't have to become a bike shop mechanic who does all their own bike maintenance. I fancy myself a pretty handy guy and do a lot of my own bike maintenance, but I still take my bikes into the shop for anything more major than a good cleaning or a small adjustment here and there. That said, every triathlete needs to know how to perform some basic bike maintenance tasks because a clean bike is a fast bike…literally.

The last thing you want to happen is to go through months and months of hard training, taking time away from family and work, only to get to race day and have the effort you put forth not make you any faster. Unfortunately, that's what's happening with a poorly tuned bike; if your bike is dirty or not running smoothly you could be putting out the same power or effort as the person beside you, but your effort is going toward grinding a chain through dirt or spinning wheels slightly off straight and you will be slower, potentially a lot slower.

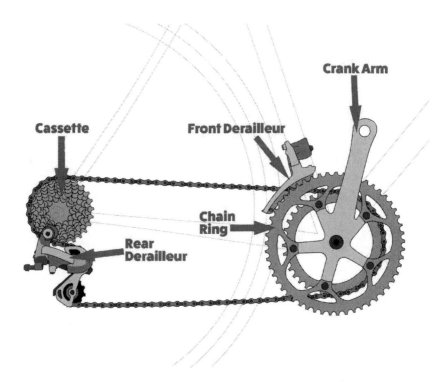

These parts comprise the drive train of a bicycle.

Here are the basic bike maintenance activities you need to learn how to perform:

- Cleaning and lubricating your entire drive train. This should be done every 2-3 weeks or after a dirty/rainy ride.
- Aligning your chain with the front chainring and the rear cassette so shifting is exact at the derailleurs don't rub.
- Removing and reinstalling your wheels so they don't rub the brake pads and they're aligned dead straight.

- Changing your tires and tubes so that you can ride a more durable tire during training to avoid flats, and switch over to a faster tire during races if that's something you want to do.
- Charging anything on your bike that needs charging like your power meter or Di2 groupset.

Every few weeks and before every race, you should perform a full drivetrain cleaning and lubrication, aligning your wheels and your shifting, charging whatever needs to be charged, and perhaps changing out to faster rubber for the race, will keep your bike as much as a few kilometers per hour faster at the same efforts. It will also make your bike last longer and reduce your lifetime repair costs.

HILL AND WIND RIDING STRATEGY

One of the most common pacing strategies triathletes use for the bike portion of their race is to attempt to evenly pace the bike without any spikes above or below the average number (power or heart rate) they're targeting for pacing. We'll talk about pacing in the next section in more depth, but that even pacing strategy creates problems in real-world conditions, resulting in slower bike times and actually worse pacing.

I'm going to lay out the common strategy athletes use for riding hills or wind (the strategy to ride them effectively is similar). Let's use an example of an athlete trying to average 200 watts (the same could be said for a target average heart rate) throughout the bike section without any spikes above or below that target figure throughout the ride.

As this athlete climbs hills or rides into the wind, to keep their target metric without spiking they must reduce their effort level. Unfortunately, this creates a big speed penalty because the athlete is no longer riding strong. Then, as the athlete goes down a hill or goes with the wind, to keep the same target metric without dropping, they must work extra hard to keep up without gaining much of a speed advantage.

TYPICAL EVEN PACE HILL STRATEGY

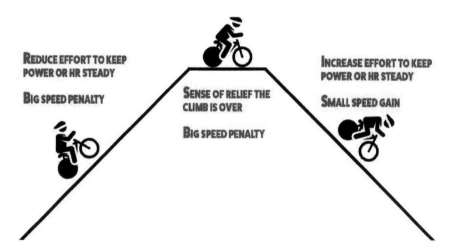

REDUCE EFFORT TO KEEP
POWER OR HR STEADY

BIG SPEED PENALTY

SENSE OF RELIEF THE
CLIMB IS OVER

BIG SPEED PENALTY

INCREASE EFFORT TO KEEP
POWER OR HR STEADY

SMALL SPEED GAIN

Instead, a better strategy for riding hills or wind is to vary your effort level but maintain the same average. When riding up hills or into the wind, let your effort level increase varying from your target average by 5-15 percent. The speed gain will be dramatic and you'll pass a lot of people who are concerned about not spiking their metric. If you're on a hill, when you crest, put in an even bigger surge of 10-20 percent to keep the speed you've built up during the climb and build speed for the descent. Then as you go onto the descent, or turn around to ride with the wind, you can let your metric decline by 5-15 percent and let gravity or the wind do most of the work for you; you'll be getting a break from the ride and won't incur much of a speed loss at all.

VARIABLE PACE HILL STRATEGY

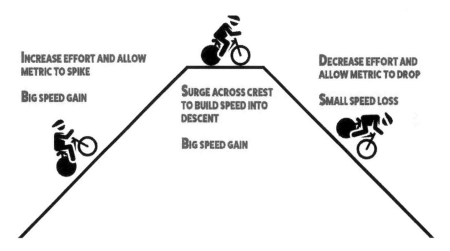

INCREASE EFFORT AND ALLOW METRIC TO SPIKE

BIG SPEED GAIN

SURGE ACROSS CREST TO BUILD SPEED INTO DESCENT

BIG SPEED GAIN

DECREASE EFFORT AND ALLOW METRIC TO DROP

SMALL SPEED LOSS

The result of this variable pace strategy will be the same average power or heart rate, but a drastically faster time. Perform this strategy over multiple hills and multiple sections, with or without the wind, and you'll be riding faster than your competitors at the same effort level.

Cameron Wurf says that he isn't even close to the most powerful or aerodynamic rider on the pro triathlon circuit, but he sets course records all around the world because his time as a pro cyclist allowed him to learn how to use the course to his advantage in ways such as this.

GEARING

The final piece you need to get right to execute a good race and let your fitness show off as much as possible is proper gearing; get it right and you'll transfer as much power to your bike as possible, get it wrong and you'll be sending a lot of power out the sides of the drivetrain, getting completely wasted. In general, you want your gearing selection to do two things:

1. Allow you to spin at a pedalling cadence that's in your comfort zone, typically between 75-95rpm, which will keep your bum stable on the saddle.
2. Result in a chain that's as straight as possible.

Accomplishing the first requirement of efficient gearing is easy, you just shift up and down until you reach a gear that provides just the right resistance to keep your target cadence on track. Your target cadence will likely be somewhere between 85-95 most of the time while it'll drop into the 70s on hill climbs, and up around 95-110 on descents.

The second requirement is gear selection, where you will need to develop some understanding of proper gearing. Let's use the example of getting into a good 90 cadence by being in the small chainring on the front and the fourth gear from the end in the back OR to get a very similar cadence by being in the big gear in the front and the sixth from the end gear in the back. That's because the gear ratios are very close to each other, generating a similar resistance and thus similar cadence.

In the case above, the first option results in a very straight chain that isn't pulled at an angle to get in the front and back gears, while the second option has the chain pulled at a big angle to get in each of the gears. The second scenario will place tension on the chain resulting in power being required to turn the pedals, making it harder on the cyclist, and energy from the chain is being transferred sideways into the bike instead of perfectly straight. Power is being lost sideways, and it's going to result in riding slower than with a straighter chain.

When in doubt about whether you should be using the big or small gear in the front, and which gear you should be using in the back, remember this rule of thumb: you first want to be in the gear that results in the right cadence that doesn't have you grinding gears or spinning, then you want to select the gear combination that results in the chain being the straightest.

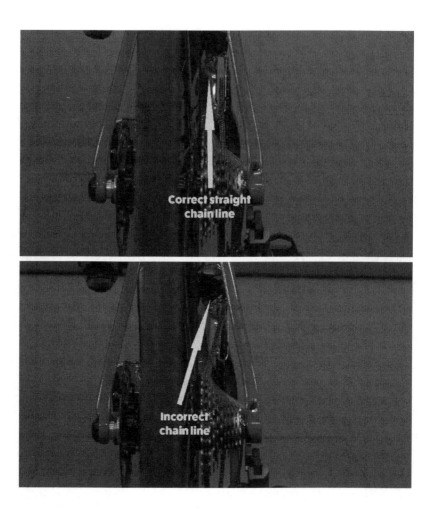

PACING

Pacing is the final piece of the puzzle in letting the work you've done throughout the year show itself off.

Pacing can make or break your race and is probably more important than anyone thinks. We interviewed Sebastian Weber on our podcast, a sports scientist and head coach of many professional cycling teams and pro triathletes, and asked him why he thought Cameron Wurf has been able to break bike course records all around the world despite not being as powerful or as aero as other riders. His answer surprised me when he said that he believes the way Cam paces a race is the deciding factor in his bike performance.

If you pace your bike section too hard, you might fade toward the end of the bike or have a bad performance on your run. The difference between a good run and a bad run could be as little as two to three minutes in a Sprint race or as much as an hour in an IRONMAN. So just bike easy to set yourself up for a good run then, right? The difference between a good bike and a bad bike isn't as drastic as the difference between a good and a bad run, but if you pace your bike too easy, you will, of course, be slower than you'd like, particularly if the bike course is hilly or windy.

The goal of pacing a triathlon bike is to find the effort level that will lead to a bad run, then dial that effort level back roughly five percent. This gets you close to the edge of your personal fastest bike split possible without sacrificing the run.

Here's how you can go about finding your unique bike pace and execute it on race day.

FINDING YOUR RACE PACE

I'd love to be able to prescribe to you a bike test that generates a result, then just say that your pace is X percent of that result for a Sprint and Y percent of that result for an IRONMAN, etc., but pacing doesn't quite work like that.

I traveled to my first IRONMAN-branded 70.3 event with a friend who was a new female pro. At the time, I was a slightly faster rider than she was and we had the same coach, but she was pacing her ride at 80 percent of her FTP (Functional Threshold Power, the max power she could theoretically hold for 60 minutes) while I was only pacing at 75 percent. Our bike times were very similar despite different capabilities and different pacing strategies.

Pacing is unique to each athlete and depends on things like fitness on the bike, weekly bike mileage, quality of recovery, length of time doing triathlons, length of training build-up, and an entire host of other variables. Here are the guidelines for rate of perceived exertion that I gave you previously, to get you started dealing in your race pace, then we'll fine-tune your pace strategy from there:

- ➤ **Sprint**: 8/10
- ➤ **Olympic**: 7/10
- ➤ **70.3**: 6-7/10
- ➤ **IRONMAN**: 6/10

Once you've calculated your heart rate zones with the Heart Rate Zone Calculator that you downloaded at triathlontaren.com/bikefoundations, you can reference your zones with this guideline for approximately where you should pace each distance race:

> **Sprint**: Middle to top of Zone 4
> **Olympic**: Bottom to middle of Zone 4
> **70.3**: Middle of Zone 3 to bottom of Zone 4
> **IRONMAN**: Top of Zone 2 to very bottom of Zone 3

Using these RPE guidelines is where you start dialing in your race pace. During those long rides in the final several months before a race where you start introducing, then increasing, the amount of time spent at race effort, you'll ride at roughly the RPE values given above. Then after the bike ride, you should perform a race simulation brick run and take note of how it feels. If your body feels stiff and doesn't loosen up, or by the end of the run you're finding your run pace drop, then it's likely the race pace effort on your bike was a little too hard so you can adjust accordingly the following week. Perform this routine week after week, and you'll develop the power to feel out your race pace without any data, like from a power meter or even via heart rate.

If you have the luxury of owning a power meter or heart rate monitor, rather than try to shove a power or heart rate number into your race pace, flip the approach and look back at the power and heart rate you were holding during your comfortable race pace efforts and you'll see the rough range that is your unique race pace.

These race pace efforts must be done at the end of a sufficiently long bike followed by a sufficiently long brick run so your legs are tired and challenged, thus allowing you to know how your legs will react on race day.

Congratulations. Not only do you know your race pace via power or heart rate, but you most importantly know it by *feel*. This is tremendously powerful because you now know how to pace a bike if you've nailed a taper and end up feeling much better than expected, or if you've traveled to a race and aren't reacting well to the deviation from your normal routine. You can use your metrics for reference but can now also make judgment calls, dialing your effort levels up and down in line with how your body is performing.

This ability to feel your race pace in conjunction with having some metrics to guide you toward your race pace is a powerful combination. Finally, you need to dose your effort throughout the race in such a way that maximizes the work you put out in a race and sets you up for success on the run.

PACING FOR A SPRINT

This will be the easiest race you'll ever pace because it's simple: one step short of blowing up the entire way. Of course, this will be a different speed and effort level for each athlete but a Sprint is so short that the pace is just a slight notch lower than a max effort. Even if you overcook the bike a bit, the run is also so short that the penalty for a poor run performance is minimal, so take a risk and push yourself into a hurt locker.

For a Sprint distance race, I recommend the following strategy after getting on your bike out of transition:

- Build up to your race effort over 1-2 minutes.
- Hold even race effort up until 2 minutes from the end of the bike.
- If you're feeling good, you can push a little extra and even "ride a little angry" because you can get away with a slight overexertion in a Sprint. The effort should feel fairly challenging.
- Stretch your lower back and legs a little bit at two minutes from the end of the bike.
- Bring your effort level down 5-10 percent from your main race effort to allow your legs to loosen up a little before getting off the bike.

PACING FOR AN OLYMPIC

Olympic triathlons are paced very similar to Sprint distance races in that they're not extremely variable; you'll build yourself up to a solid race pace effort and hold it. The race pace effort of an Olympic distance triathlon, however, is one notch lower than a Sprint distance race.

While a Sprint is so short that an athlete can still have a great performance even with overreached effort levels, an Olympic distance race is a long enough bike and run that you could fade significantly in both if you push too hard. So, dial back the effort just a bit from Sprint race pace and be careful not to overreach; when in doubt, be more cautious.

For an Olympic distance race, I recommend the following strategy after getting on your bike out of transition:

- Build up to your race effort over 2-3 minutes.
- Hold even race effort up until 3 minutes from the end of the bike.
- Try not to over-exert yourself on the bike even if you're feeling good. The effort should be strong, but not difficult.
- Stretch your lower back and legs a little bit at 3 minutes from the end of the bike.
- Bring your effort level down 5-10 percent from your main race effort to allow your legs to loosen up a little before getting off the bike.

PACING FOR A 70.3

Pacing a half-IRONMAN, now officially known as a 70.3, is where getting your pace dialed in, and controlling that pace throughout the ride to set yourself up for a strong run, becomes quite critical. An error in your race pace can lead to a significantly longer bike and a suffer-fest throughout the entire run.

Until you've got an excellent handle on where the fine line between just the right amount of effort and too much effort is, the effort level for a 70.3 is quite measured. Your best plan is to hold yourself back in races. As you develop more body awareness, more race knowledge, and get several years of miles in your legs, you'll be able to "fly closer to the sun" and race closer to the top end of your physical abilities, but until that time it's a better strategy to hold yourself back.

For a 70.3 distance race, I recommend the following strategy after getting on your bike out of transition:

- Build up to just slightly under race effort over 5-7 minutes.
- For the first third of the bike, be cautious and think about riding at 3-5 percent under what you believe your race effort should feel like to get a handle on where your body is at on race day.
- At one third into the bike, if you're feeling good, bring your effort level up to race effort and hold it.
- As the race goes on, have regular check-ins with your body. If you're feeling like the effort is too hard, you

should dial it back. If the effort level feels too easy, you should probably just maintain the effort.

- During the final third of the bike leg, decide how your body is feeling. If you feel absolutely, stupendously, AMAZING you can bring your effort level up to just a touch above the race effort you've been holding. But if you just feel adequate, stick with your target race effort level into the end of the ride.

- Stretch your lower back and legs a couple of times, even sit up a bit to make sure you're comfortable in the final 10 minutes from the end of the bike.

- During the final 3-5 minutes, bring your effort level down 5-10 percent from your main race effort to allow your legs to loosen up a little before getting off the bike.

PACING FOR AN IRONMAN

An IRONMAN is the most critical race distance to pace conservatively. The difference between a great and a poor bike performance during an IRONMAN could be as much as 30 minutes, but the difference between a good and a bad run could be an hour or more. We want to be extra cautious in an IRONMAN distance race to give ourselves every opportunity to have a solid run that doesn't turn into a six-hour death march.

I keep referring to Cam Wurf throughout this book, not because he's such an incredible beast on the bike, but because he's one of the smartest riders in triathlon and he can get the most out of the bike fitness he has. To give you some context of how different the effort level is between 70.3 and IRONMAN: Cam Wurf looks to hold 380 watts over the course of a 70.3 (very close to his FTP) but just 300 watts over the course of an IRONMAN. This is a huge drop in the effort level between the two races, do likewise.

For an IRONMAN distance race, I recommend the following strategy after getting on your bike out of transition:

- Build up to just slightly under race effort over 5-7 minutes.
- For the first half of the bike, be cautious and think about riding at 3-5 percent under what you believe your race effort should feel like, to get a handle on where your body is at on race day.
- At the halfway mark into the bike, if you're feeling good, bring your effort level up to race effort and hold it.
- As the race goes on, have regular check-ins with your body. If you're feeling like the effort is too hard, you should dial it back. If the effort level feels too easy, you should probably just maintain the effort.
- During the final third of the bike leg, decide how your body is feeling. If you feel absolutely, stupendously, AMAZING you can bring your effort level up to just a touch above the race effort you've been holding. But if

you just feel adequate, stick with your target race effort level into the end of the ride.

- Stretch your lower back and legs a couple of times, even sit up a bit to make sure you're comfortable in the final 10 minutes from the end of the bike.
- During the final 5-10 minutes bring your effort level down 5-10 percent from your main race effort to allow your legs to loosen up a little before getting off the bike.

VARIABLE PACING

Finally, I want to drive home the point I made when I discussed the hill and wind riding strategy. The race pacing guidelines I just outlined talk about even pacing. What I mean is, roughly even pacing within a range.

Use the hill and wind riding strategy and feel free to allow your effort level to vary slightly upward and downward on hills and in the wind, but overall keep the average effort level in mind. I once heard a race pace strategy described by a pro quite simply as, "Try to stay between 275 and 325 watts and don't go over 400 watts too many times." This gives you an idea of how the target average race pace is just an average with some variability, but you just need to manage the severe spikes.

CHAPTER 9

PUSHING OFF

RIDING OFF INTO THE SUNSET

I know that the bike can be the most intimidating discipline in triathlon, but I hope this three-part system of optimizing your bike, then optimizing your workouts, then optimizing your strength, gives you the confidence to make the entire bike leg your strength.

While the triathlon bike can be expensive and time-consuming, it doesn't have to be. Select only the gear that you can afford, and hopefully the guide we've given you here provides the knowledge of what the best purchases are for you. With the two key workouts a week system, I hope you'll now be able to focus on high return workouts that get you to Transition 1 feeling strong.

The great thing about the bike leg of a triathlon is that it's the easiest discipline of the three sports to turn into a weapon and a strong part of your athletic talent. Swimming takes years (if ever) to become elite at, and running is often dependent upon natural biomechanics and the "How easily do you get injured lottery." However, every single triathlete can become an excellent rider, it just takes time in the saddle, focused on the right things.

The very first Olympic distance race I ever did was my third triathlon, just a 40 km bike in some moderate hills that even athletes in the 65-plus age categories were able to tackle. But this race was awful for me. My bike time and overall time were dead last in my age category, and I finished at the very back of the overall race. My bike was poorly maintained, the chain squeaked, I didn't use aerobars, it was the first time I had ridden 40 km, and I had never biked much harder than a commuting-to-work kind of effort. I did everything wrong.

Men 25-29

Place	Total	Bib #	Competitor	City	Swim	Bike	Run
1	2:16:41	382	Les FRIESEN	Steinbach	28:08	1:10:37	37:57
2	2:34:36	388	Christopher SCHWEITZER	Regina	26:27	1:20:57	47:13
3	2:36:45	52	Mathieu BROSSEAU	Brandon	30:42	1:24:01	42:03
4	2:42:19	444	Scott BEATON	Winnipeg	26:05	1:24:47	51:28
5	3:04:58	409	Taren GESELL	Winnipeg	41:31	1:31:34	51:54

2010 Riding Mountain Triathlon Results

Fast forward to 2019 at the IRONMAN 70.3 in Puerto Rico, my bike split was 2:18 and the sixth fastest overall out of 1200 athletes from all around the world. In 2018, I did an Olympic distance race just for training and put out a 2:12, finishing third overall, far away from the near last place 3:04 I put up in 2010. Sure, in 2019 I had a much nicer bike but I upgraded to that bike slowly over nine years as I had the funds to do so, and it wasn't like I had some underlying bike talent that just wasn't there on the Olympic race day in 2010, because even as I started riding with groups in 2015, I was spectacularly average.

Instead, what allowed me to make such significant gains on the bike over the years was just consistently chipping away at the right workouts time after time, and gradually, but without fail, I got faster and faster. You will too!

So, what is it going to take for you to get faster on the bike, or even just to get to your race confident and across the finish line feeling strong? I believe you can easily get there by doing just three things and doing them consistently:

1. Get in these two bike workouts each week; one quite challenging workout and one less intense longer workout.
2. Prioritize recovery, making sure you get seven or more hours of sleep most nights and eat well, ensuring your body has the time to get faster or stronger, and the right materials to rebuild you into a total triathlon badass.

3. Repeat steps 1 and 2 week after week, month after month, year after year. There's almost no way that if you're challenging yourself enough, and giving your body what it needs to recover, that you won't make more progress and achieve things that you never thought possible.

You have also seen me mention the website TeamTrainiac.com throughout this book, which is our online triathlon coaching website where athletes get year-round, customized training plans including swim, bike, run, and strength training, all based on when and how much you specifically want to train.

While I'm very partial to it and think it's a great option for any triathlete from beginner to advanced (I used the plan when training for the 4:35 I did in the 2018 70.3 World Championship), I think it's an even better option for developing triathletes who wouldn't consider themselves advanced. We make the workouts easily accessible to athletes at all levels, simple to understand, have video and audio explanations of parts of the workout for clarity, and it's a damn good group of triathletes who you get to interact with as you encourage each other in your training in our Team Trainiac social media feed.

That said, it doesn't have to be Team Trainiac that you use for your training. It can be a local triathlon club, go at it self-coached, or hire a one-on-one coach. Regardless which option you choose, the same three principles above will apply so make sure that no matter what option you choose to use for your training that you're getting in good workouts with the principles we've outlined here. You never sacrifice sleep and nutrition for your overall health, thinking it's the price you need to pay for training. If you ever reach a point where you're putting in plenty of work but not seeing yourself make improvements, then come back to this book and see where your boat might have a leak.

Most importantly, as you go forward make sure you enjoy triathlon! Triathletes can be very hard on themselves, training and racing despite a lack of motivation for the sport or to the detriment of their work-family-health balance. Don't ever feel like you HAVE TO always be crushing personal bests, or that you HAVE TO always be stepping up to bigger and bigger races. Sometimes your life will allow you to purchase more gear or spend a year doing huge amounts of training for a longer race, but don't let that feeling that you HAVE TO always be making progress take away from the enjoyment of the sport.

In the end, triathlon is a hobby that we all need to have fun doing. If that means limiting our purchases to only what we can afford, great! If that means doing less training than I've outlined here while being okay that it might just lead to a less than perfect race, that's fine too. Only do as much or as little as is comfortable and realistic for you, just have the perspective of where you're at. Judge yourself only by the quality of the work you put in given your unique circumstances, and not by the finish time you achieve or the amount of gear you have.

Enjoy the journey, have fun, and make new friends!

CHAPTER 10

HIIT WORKOUTS

12 HIIT WORKOUTS

Below is a sample of 12 workouts that we use on TeamTrainiac.com that can be used for any race distance you might be training for. HIIT training isn't about accumulating volume; rather, it's about accumulating intensity and, specifically, it's about accumulating a solid number of repetitions bursting out of low intensity to high intensity.

These workouts can take anywhere from 20-50 minutes, so most of our athletes choose to do them during the week when time is limited, and a very efficient and effective workout is needed.

The workouts below are based off of Zones, which recommend using the rate of perceived exertion zones when doing HIIT training. Heart rate doesn't work well for HIIT training because heart rate lags and intervals might be so short that the heart rate won't ever get into the prescribed zone within the time of the interval. Power zones are fine for HIIT training, but I find when you're going REALLY intensely, you're not looking at power numbers.

GUIDELINES FOR RATE OF PERCEIVED EXERTION ZONES

Zone 1: 1-2 out of 10 effort level. This could be to the physical exertion of a brisk walk. This Zone tends to be used strictly for recovery within a workout immediately after a really hard effort, or during total recovery workouts.

Zone 2: 3-4 out of 10 effort level. This is your sweet spot for aerobic fitness building. It's also a great effort level to flush lactic acid from legs.

Zone 3: 5-6 out of 10 effort level. This is a race pace or long "solid" workout effort level. It's just hard enough to feel like a good effort but not so difficult that it can't be sustained for a long workout. This would be compared to a half marathon effort level.

Zone 4: 7-8 out of 10 effort level. This is quite a challenging effort level that can only be sustained for 5-20 minutes. It can be compared to a 5 km running race effort level, very difficult! This effort level builds up your top end of aerobic fitness, your VO2 Max.

Zone 5: 9-10 out of 10 effort level. This is where we get into building pure speed, power, muscle strength, durability, ability to turn muscles over quickly, tolerate pain. This is a very hard effort level and would be compared to a 400-1600m interval on the track.

MAX EFFORT: In workouts, we often have "Max Effort" indicated, which is simply the maximum effort level you can hold for the prescribed period without a significant drop off in effort by the end of the interval. This means "max effort" will be higher for a 30-second interval than it will be for a two minute "max effort."

BASE SEASON WORKOUT #1

This can be used when you're coming out of the off-season and want to start getting the body acclimated to more intense bursts. The purpose is to just give the body a small taste of intensity to ease into HIIT training.

Warm-up:

- 5 minutes easy spinning
- 5 minutes progressive warmup, increasing one gear every minute
- 3 minutes Zone 2 recovery spinning

Repeat this main set five times:

- 45 seconds building gradually from Zone 2 to max effort, seated sprint for final 10 seconds
- 45 seconds recovery spin
- 45 seconds building gradually from Zone 2 to max effort, standing sprint for final 10 seconds
- 45 seconds recovery spin

Cool down:

- 3 minutes easy recovery spin

BASE SEASON WORKOUT #2

This is a hill riding effort workout. The fastest hill riding strategy is to push 5-10 percent harder than your target average race effort going up the hill, pushing 10-20 percent harder as you crest the hill, then carry that speed and coast at 5-10 percent under your target average race effort going down the hill. This results in approximately the same average power expenditure but a massive time savings over holding constant effort throughout. This workout isn't yet terribly intense as you're still in the base fitness building portion of the season.

Warm-up:

- 10 minutes building from an easy spin to Zone 2

Repeat the below 75-second hill cresting simulation five times:

- Shift onto big chainring and a middle/end cog. Over 5-10 seconds, build steadily up to a hard effort "reaching the top of the hill."
- Over the next 5-10 seconds, stand and surge slightly, "reaching the hilltop flats."
- Then, hold steady power of Zone 4 hard effort for the remainder of the 75 second interval simulating "holding the speed across the top of the hill."
- Drop down to a Zone 2 steady spin, keeping tension on the chain for 45 seconds, "coasting down the hill maintaining the speed you built cresting the hill".

Cool down:

- 5 minutes easy recovery spin

BASE SEASON WORKOUT #3

This is where we start adding quite intense efforts to the workouts toward the end of the base fitness building season.

Warm-up:

- 7 minutes building from easy spin to Zone 2.

Repeat the following 3-minute sequence seven times:

- 30 seconds Zone 2
- Then 20 seconds Zone 4
- Then 10 second max effort
- 2 minutes at Zone 2, to flush lactic acid from legs
- Repeat that four more times

Cool-down:

- 2 minutes easy spin

BASE SEASON WORKOUT #4

This is a workout to be used toward the end of the base fitness building part of your season; you can see that it has some REALLY intense efforts and it will be quite challenging. We want to build up to completing this workout so don't jump into doing 30-second max efforts right from the start.

Warm-up:

- 5 minutes easy spin
- 5 minutes efficient bike warmup, with 6-second build to sprint at the beginning of every minute

Repeat 5 times:

- 30 seconds building to absolutely max-effort (MAX MAX MAX, near throwing-up) for final 10 seconds
- Take 30 seconds to compose yourself
- 1 minute of light spinning
- 1 minute of Zone 2 recovery spin

Cool-down:

- 4 minutes easy recovery spin, gradually dropping down from Zone 2 to easy spinning at the end

STRENGTH & SPEED SEASON WORKOUT #1

In this workout, we start introducing differing cadence cycling so you're combining hard efforts with strength-based efforts. Notice how the low-cadence cycling isn't yet intense, we want to acclimate your body to low-cadence work as it places a lot of torque on the muscles and joints so we need to adapt gradually.

Warm-up:

- 5 minutes, easy spin
- 5 minutes, progress one gear every minute, maintaining cadence

Repeat five times:

- 10-second all-out maximal-effort sprint

- 1:50 low cadence (60-70) with low-intensity Zone 2 recovery

Repeat five times:

- 15 seconds all-out maximal-effort sprint
- 1:45 low cadence (60-70) with low-intensity Zone 2 recovery

STRENGTH & SPEED SEASON WORKOUT #2

Notice how this workout is identical to the previous workout, but the intense intervals are longer while the rest interval is shorter. I've included this workout to show that as you progress through workouts, they don't have to be radically different to keep the body guessing, they just need to be progressively more and more challenging, which is enough of a different stimulus to keep the body in a progressive state of adaptation.

Warm-up:

- 5 minutes, easy spin
- 5 minutes, progress one gear every minute, maintaining cadence

Repeat five times:

- 20 seconds all-out maximal-effort sprint
- 1:40 low cadence (60-70) with low-intensity Zone 2 recovery

Repeat five times:

- 25 seconds all-out maximal-effort sprint
- 1:35 low cadence (60-70) with low-intensity Zone 2 recovery

STRENGTH & SPEED SEASON WORKOUT #3

This Russian sprint workout is one of the most challenging efforts you'll do because, as you get tired, the hard intervals get longer and the rest intervals get shorter, compounding the fatigue. You'll find that the effort levels at the end will be markedly lower efforts than at the start, and that's okay because the purpose is to push through that fatigue.

Warm up:

- 5 minutes, easy spin
- 4x10-second Zone 4
- 20 seconds easy spin
- 3 minutes at Zone 2

Repeat this Russian Sprint pyramid 1-2 times (stay seated for entire set):

- 5-second sprint/55-second easy spin
- 10-second sprint/50-second easy spin
- 15-second sprint/45-second easy spin
- 20-second Sprint/40-second easy spin
- 25-second sprint/35-second easy spin
- 30-second sprint/30-second easy spin

- 35-second sprint/25-second easy spin
- 40-second sprint/20-second easy spin
- 45-second sprint/15-second easy spin
- 3-minute recovery spin

STRENGTH & SPEED SEASON WORKOUT #4

This workout is similar to the Russian sprints with a slight variation in that, as fatigue builds up, you return to getting a little more rest. This allows a little more recovery so that you can dig a little deeper toward the end and maintain high effort levels.

Warm-up:

- 10 minutes, building from easy to Zone 2

Repeat twice:

- 15-second Max effort/ 45-second easy recovery
- 30-second Max effort/ 30-second easy recovery
- 45-second Max effort/ 15-second easy recovery
- 30-second Max effort/ 30-second easy recovery
- 15-second Max effort/ 45-second easy recovery
- 10 minutes cooling down from Zone 2 to easy spinning

RACE SEASON WORKOUT #1

In this workout, we're combining longer sustained efforts that are more similar to the race season with strength-based cycling via the low cadence workout, while including a burst of hard effort riding to keep that top end challenge.

Warm-up:

- 5-minute building from easy to Zone 2

Repeat twice:

- 3 minutes building from Zone 2 to Zone 4 for final 15 seconds
- 1 minute of easy spinning
- 90 seconds low (40-60) cadence Zone 2
- 90 seconds low (40-60) cadence Zone 3
- 90 seconds low (40-60) cadence Zone 4
- 15 seconds low (40-60) cadence low Zone 5
- 15 seconds stand up out of saddle and EXPLODE with an absolute max-effort high cadence, as hard as you can possibly go
- 5-minute easy spin
- 5-minute cool down

RACE SEASON WORKOUT #2:

This workout provides a challenge to the body by exercising the ends of range cadences at the low cadence and the high cadence, then stresses the body with a longer, harder effort. We're building the ability to pedal at all cadences and at fast efforts, breaking you out of just steady riding over and over.

Warm-up:

- 5 minutes building from easy to Zone 2

Repeat five times:

- 15 seconds at Zone 4/5 then 45-second easy spin
- 3 minutes easy spinning

Repeat five times:

- 3 minutes low cadence (50-70) Zone 2
- 2 minutes high (100) cadence Zone 2
- 1 minute at Zone 4/5 hard-effort regular cadence
- 2-minute cool down

RACE SEASON WORKOUT #3

Notice how we're extending the amount of time spent at very hard efforts? This will naturally cause the hard to be more moderate than a 15-second sprint and will be in the high Zone 4 area, pushing up the top end of VO2 Max and top end of aerobic fitness.

Warm-up:

- 5 minutes easy spinning

Repeat twice:

- 15 seconds Zone 4
- 45 seconds Zone 2
- 3 minutes spinning at Zone 2, to flush lactic acid from legs

Main Set:

- 1 minute very hard/ 30 seconds easy
- 1 minute very hard/ 30 seconds easy
- 2 minutes very hard/ 1 minute easy
- 2 minutes very hard/ 1 minute easy
- 1 minute very hard/ 90 seconds easy
- 1 minute very hard/ 90 seconds easy
- 30 seconds very hard/ 2 minutes easy/ 30 seconds very hard/ 2 minutes easy

RACE SEASON WORKOUT #4:

This workout is a longer sustained effort that isn't terribly intense, rather it's a race simulation kind of workout. You should notice that as the season progresses, workouts change from dissimilar to a race to more and more similar to a race.

Warm-up:

- 5 minutes easy spin
- 3 minutes building one gear each minute, ending at Zone 3

Main set (ideally, stay in aerobars the entire time):

- Ride for 30 minutes mainly at race pace with race cadence

- Every three minutes, perform 30 seconds high Zone 4 (50-70) cadence, then drop down to 30 seconds Zone 2 at high (+100) cadence

Cool-down:

- 2 minutes

An important thing to understand about HIIT training is that there is no clear "secret sauce" that's been identified by researchers as far as the length of interval, duration of rest interval, exact intensity, etc. The key points to nail if you're creating your own HIIT workouts are:

The intense interval has to be a quite intense, top-end kind of effort that's really challenging.

The rest interval should be just barely enough to feel like you can start the next hard interval but not so long that you're totally recovered.

Intense intervals become longer and intensity goes down as the season progresses toward race season.

Based on how you're feeling rest week, HIIT workouts can be simply a version of the workouts you do during your non-rest weeks with fewer intervals. Or, if you're feeling extremely fatigued during rest week, you want to dial back the intensity.

Taper week HIIT workouts still maintain strong efforts, just fewer. So, if you built up to doing 6x3 minutes hard efforts leading up to a race, you'd do 3x3 minutes during a taper week.

Remember that these types of intense bike workouts are quite taxing on the system and need to be carefully placed within a training week. Make sure that you're not risking sickness, overtraining, burnout, or even just doing a lot of hard work without getting much return from it, by using the spreadsheet called Triathlon Training Plan Calculator at our website, triathlontaren.com/bikefoundations. That's where you'll see where you should place the intense ride during the week, based on how many times a week you work out.

DEFINITIONS

CHAINRING: A chainring is the round, spiky disc connected to the cranks that pulls the chain around.

FRONT/REAR DERAILLEUR: The derailleur is the device that changes gears by moving the chain from one sprocket to another. There are two derailleurs, one on the rear and one on the front.

DRIVETRAIN: The drivetrain of a bike consists of all of the mechanical parts that push the bike forward (pedals, cranks, chainrings, chain, cassette, and derailleurs.)

GROUPO/GRUPPO: See Groupset.

GROUPSET: A groupset refers to any mechanical or electronic parts involved in braking, changing gears or the running of the drivetrain. This includes the shifters, the brake levers, the front and rear brake calipers, the front and rear derailleurs, the crankset, the chain, the chainring, and the cassette.

REAR CASSETTE: A bicycle cassette is the cluster of sprockets located on the rear hub of your bike; it is the other half of the mechanism with the chainring, where the chain sits.

SADDLE: A saddle is a bike seat.

SADDLE FORE & AFT: Fore-aft or fore and aft positioning relates to the distance between your seat and handlebars.

SPLIT-NOSE SADDLE: A split-nose saddle is a saddle that's split at the front.

TT POSITION: Time trial position.

TYRE: Common spelling of the word "tire" in cycling lingo.

ACKNOWLEDGMENTS

To the Tuesday/Thursday morning ride group, thank you for helping me learn to handle my bike like a true road cyclist.

To Rod, still sorry for running you off the road and breaking your rib.

To James and the gang at Alter Ego, thank you for the countless fixes, tune-ups, and great care you've taken with every bike I've brought in for repair.

To Jimmy, Diaa, Rachel, and the entire Ventum family, thank you for supporting a young upstart with your beautiful machines. I'm proud to ride your bikes.

And thanks to my wife Kim for not only riding alongside me on my Sunday morning long runs as I prepared for my first Iron-distance race, but for always riding alongside me in life.

WHAT'S NEXT

Now that you're done with this book, here are some next steps for you.

1. JOIN THE TRAINIAC COMMUNITY

There are so many ways to join the Trainiac community! Here's how:

Visit us online at <u>triathlontaren.com</u> for free resources, valuable training info, and more.

Visit <u>TeamTrainiac.com</u> to get signed up to the most accessible triathlon training platform in the world. For a fraction of the price of a one-on-one coach, get a fully customizable, year-round training plan to get you totally prepared for your races, no matter your level of experience!

Visit **protriathlontraining.com** to take your triathlon game to the next level with training advice, tips and tricks from some of the top professional triathletes and coaches in the world. Easy-to-follow modules will help you make game-changing tweaks and improvements to the way you race.

2. FOLLOW US ON SOCIAL MEDIA

For tips, tricks, training updates and more, follow us on our most active social media channels:

YOUTUBE: youtube.com/triathlontaren

INSTAGRAM: @triathlontaren

FACEBOOK: facebook.com/triathlontaren

3. SUBSCRIBE TO THE TRIATHLON TAREN PODCAST

The top-rated Triathlon podcast in the world on iTunes, the Triathlon Taren podcast brings you interviews with the who's-who in triathlon including professional triathletes, inspiring age-groupers and more! Download the podcast wherever you get your favorite podcasts.

4. SHARE THIS BOOK

Please write us a review on Amazon and let your fellow triathletes know about us! Spreading the word helps to reach new readers, to grow the Trainiac community, and it allows us to bring you more great resources.

THANK YOU! And we'll see ya soon, Trainiac!

ABOUT THE AUTHOR

"Triathlon Taren" Gesell is a triathlete who has become known for his wildly popular Triathlon Taren YouTube page, Instagram account and podcast, where he shares tips, tricks, hacks and time-tested knowledge to help age-groupers get to their start lines confident and their finish lines strong. Based in Winnipeg, Canada, Triathlon Taren is also the head coach of Team Trainiac, a training platform supporting a growing community of triathletes from all around the world.

Find more books by "TRIATHLON TAREN" GESELL on Amazon.com

Made in the USA
Middletown, DE
07 March 2020